The
Desperate Housewife's
Guide to
Life and Love

THIS IS A CARLTON BOOK

Text, design and illustrations copyright © 2006
Carlton Books Limited

This edition published by
Carlton Books Limited 2006
20 Mortimer Street
London W1T 3JW

A CIP catalogue record for this book is available from
the British Library.

ISBN-10 1 84442 331 X
ISBN-13 978 1 84442 331 6
ISBN (without flaps) 1 84442 203 8

Printed and bound in China

Executive Editor: Lisa Dyer
Art Editor: Zoë Dissell
Design: Liz Wiffen
Copy Editor: Gillian Holmes
Illustrator: Robyn Neild
Production: Caroline Alberti

The information and opinions contained within this book are
advisory only and may be of general interest to the reader.
This book is not a subsitute for professional advice on health,
dieting or physical fitness. It is advisable to consult your doctor
before embarking on any health or beauty regime, particularly
if you are, or suspect you may be, pregnant.

The Desperate Housewife's Guide to Life and Love

Caroline Jones

CARLTON
BOOKS

Contents

Introduction

This book goes out to desperate wives and mothers everywhere – those women who are trying to balance the pressures of life, home and family every day, in an increasingly complex and stressful world. At last, here is a complete survivor's guide to motherhood, house maintenance, fashion, work, love and kids. You'll find plenty of practical tips that are guaranteed to make your life easier and happier. So, whether you are working full-time, part-time or are a stay-at-home mother, help is at hand to make your life run more smoothly. This book is packed with advice on every dilemma facing a modern-day desperate housewife, from what to do if your husband fancies the nanny or your new boss at work is younger than you, to anti-ageing tips and coping with a late baby in your 40s.

Every chapter recognizes that while you love your partner and kids and enjoy working, as rewarding as all that can be, life becomes a misery if you can't have a little fun and let your hair down once in a while. And by the same token, just because you have hit your 30s and 40s and have more responsibilities, it doesn't mean you don't want to look glamorous and feel sexy anymore. So read on to put a little balance and joy back into your daily grind, de-frump your look, and go from desperate to dynamite in just six chapters!

Which Type Are You?

The **key to self-knowledge** is identifying the traps and unhealthy life habits you've allowed yourself to fall into. Although no one is completely one type of person or another, you might identify more strongly with one or two of the housewife types listed here. Whatever your modus operandi – laidback liberal, pull-your-hair-out neurotic mess, prissy miss perfect or do-it-all achiever – the following pages will help you examine what is working well in your life and discover the areas that need a bit more effort.

 The **Harassed** Mother

STYLE: You've gone from sharp suits to last-years jeans and a T-shirt.

CAREER: You've given up the fast-paced business world for the mess and chaos of family life – and are finding the transition tough but also rewarding.

SEX LIFE: Often too tired to even think about sex by the end of the day.

DESPERATION: Your kids. You may have happily given up work to raise them but being a mother has depleted your resources and left you feeling a little resentful.

SOLUTION: Find (or pay) a friend who'll take them for one afternoon a week and use that time to see a film, swim, etc. The break will make you a more loving and patient mom. Your kids' needs should not always come before time with your partner. Book in 'couple' time when they're asleep, switch the TV off and talk over a bottle of wine.

The **Man-eater**

STYLE: Whatever skimpy number you're wearing on top, we can be sure you're wearing Agent Provocateur lingerie underneath.

CAREER: None to speak off – chasing men is your main past time.

SEX LIFE: Yes please, and lots of it. You're outrageously flirtatious and very in touch with your sexual needs.

DESPERATION: Your out-of-control libido. There's a good chance you're confusing sexual desire with a need for love and affection, and you may tend to leap from one disastrous love affair right into another.

SOLUTION: Take time to get to know a potential partner before jumping between the sheets – it will increase your chances of finding a longer-term relationship.

★ Bored Trophy Bride

STYLE: It has to be designer and ridiculously expensive or you wouldn't be seen dead in it. Think Versace, Valentino and D&G.

CAREER: Lunching and shopping. You have a wealthy husband who takes care of all the finances.

SEX LIFE: Bored with never seeing your workaholic husband, you've seriously contemplated having an affair.

DESPERATION: Your loneliness. You may be materially well-off, but deep down your know there's more for you.

SOLUTION: Consider doing voluntary work. List your talents and match them to your favourite charities.

★ Stepford Wife

STYLE: Think spotless twinset and pearls teamed with sensible court shoes.

CAREER: Obsessive domestic goddess who feels anxious if the slightest thing is out of place, or if every evening meal isn't a spectacular culinary delight.

SEX LIFE: Sex has its place, but only if all the housework is done and it doesn't mess up the freshly laundered sheets.

DESPERATION: Your perfectionism. Your whole life is geared to being the perfect wife and mother, but because life isn't perfect, you're constantly disappointed. You have to remember that a sparkling kitchen won't solve underlying emotional problems.

SOLUTION: Let your children and partner help you with the cooking and around the house – they'll feel more involved and more inclined to support you.

★ Vulnerable Divorcee

STYLE: Sexy in a slightly dishevelled, but cool way.

CAREER: A single mother juggling work and kids.

SEX LIFE: You're in constant search of a good man, but find the whole world of dating intimidating.

DESPERATION: Your relationship, or lack of one. You crave passion, support and affection, but have no idea where to look for it.

SOLUTION: Don't sit around waiting for Mr Right and letting life pass you by. Focus on enjoying your life as it is – time with your kids, fun, friendships and girls' nights out, and going to cultural or social events you really enjoy and find fulfilling.

CHAPTER 1

Love and Sex for Real Women

Spring-clean Your Love Life

Whoever said that once you found Mr Right everything would fall into place – and stay that way – was lying. Even if you do manage to stay together, **keeping your alive is damn hard work.**

Perhaps you find yourself rowing all the time; or your sex life has lost its sparkle; or maybe you've found yourself drooling over that gorgeous guy at work once too often. The truth is the stresses and strains of juggling family life, friends and a career can make it all too **easy for your relationship to go a bit stale.** So, first things first, it is time to take stock of your love life.

Just as you accumulate junk in your house, **relationships collect baggage.** And just as spring-cleaning clears out unwanted rubbish and restores harmony to your living space, regular cleansing sessions in your relationship will refresh your love and restore the spark between you and your partner.

Step 1 DETOX TIME

If you've been together for a while, it is probably time for a thorough relationship detox. The following exercise is a good method for doing just that.

1 **Book a weekend** where the two of you can be alone and undisturbed for two whole days – leave the kids with your parents if need be.

2 **Each take a notepad** and be prepared to share the contents.

3 **Take time to write honest** endings to the following statements:
   I am with you because…
   My feelings were hurt when…
   I'm angry when…
   I resent you when…
   You always…
   You never…

Then either show or tell each other what you've written. The goal is to discuss the **tiniest resentments and hurts** that you have stored up for however long you two have been together. **Then forget it.**

One of **the worst things we all do is continuously bring up past hurts.** But this is one of the most destructive behaviours possible within a relationship and can damage even the closest couples.

Stored resentments usually happen because the difficult issues were not dealt with when they first occurred. So, next time a problem crops up, try to make sure that you get angry, argue, and do whatever you need to in order to deal with the issue – then be done with it. Forgive (if of course, it is something forgivable!) and **consign the argument to history.**

Step 2 THE POSITIVE BIT!

Take time to write endings to the following statements:

I forgive you completely for. . .
I appreciate your. . .
I thank you for. . .
You turn me on when. . .
I am proud of you because. . .
I love you because. . .

Then, as before, **share your answers** with each other.

By the time you have finished **you should feel closer,** as if you've resolved some old grudges and been reminded of all the reasons why you got together in the first place.

It might sound a bit cheesy, but **once you get in the habit of talking about how you feel** it will come more naturally. This should eventually help put an end to hidden agendas, suppressed feelings and resentments.

Restoring That Va Va Voom!

For most couples, the **barometer for how happy you feel** about your relationship is how things are in the bedroom.

If your sex life is exciting and fun, chances are everything else is going well. But **when there is trouble between the sheets**, it is usually an indication that something is wrong between the two of you.

The good news is that, with a little care and attention, it's easy to get back that loving feeling – and strengthen your relationship in the process. Here's how to tackle **the five most common problems** that hamper your sex life.

1 TOO TIRED, TOO BUSY, TOO ANYTHING

Stress and exhaustion are the number one passion killers. If you haven't got time for sex, chances are you haven't got the time or energy for other things you enjoy in life.

What to do

Give yourself some vital 'me' time to relax and look after number one – eat well, sleep well and exercise. The happier you are, the happier you'll be with someone else.

2 KIDS ARE RUINING YOUR SEX LIFE

It's perfectly normal not to want sex for up to six months after giving birth. But there comes a point when you have to make a conscious effort to make your relationship a priority again.

What to do

Get a babysitter and go out alone so you can start shifting some of the attention from your child back to your partner. A good time to reclaim your sexual body is once you stop breastfeeding.

3 LACK OF **IMAGINATION**

The fact is most women get more turned on through stimulation of their brain – not their body parts.

What to do

Explore what turns you on. Read erotic books, fantasize, experiment and masturbate. If you've never used one before, a vibrator may help to find your really erogenous zones.

4 FEELING **PRESSURED**

When you do feel ready for sex, don't rush things.

What to do

Massage is a good starting point because it's not threatening. Enjoy the intimacy and if it turns into something more exciting then that's a bonus. Have sex less often and make it more special when you do.

5 STUCK **IN A RUT**

Contrary to the Hollywood myth, relationships get boring sometimes. But this isn't a sign to break up – in fact this is the time to work hardest. So, put in the same amount of effort as when you started seeing each other.

What to do

Go out on day trips and dinner dates. Spend some time making yourself look and feel gorgeous. And spend time together doing intimate things that don't always result in sex.

Planned romantic weekends away often end in disaster because of the expectations involved, whereas a weekend that has been set aside as just for time together often leads to spontaneous love-making.

Reserving quality time for each other is vital so do get away but put the emphasis on talking and being together, not sex.

FIVE INSTANT WAYS to boost your relationship

1 **Healthy relationships begin with healthy self-esteem.** If you don't love yourself, you'll find it hard to believe your partner does. Build your self-confidence by asking your partner to list your positive attributes – now commit them to memory.

2 **Do something today for your partner** that has no purpose other than to make them happy, not because it had to be done or because it's your job to do it. Sometimes love is simply about giving and not expecting something in return.

3 **Physical contact is key**, and I don't just mean sex. When we touch, we release oxytocin – nature's bonding chemical. The more you touch, the closer you'll feel. Make sure you incorporate physical affection into your daily life, whether it's a cuddle on the sofa or a hug before you leave for work.

4 **Take a few moments to go back in time** and remember the three top reasons why you fell in love with your partner.

5 **If you've got kids, sit down with your partner** and write down a list of all the things you love most about them. Now pin those words on the notice-board and look at them whenever either of you find yourselves struggling with the many challenges that children bring.

How Not to Be Defined by Your Single Status

If it is so great to be single, why am I lonely? These days being single no longer simply means being an old maid or a spinster, but anyone who is living a life without a committed partner. When you were married or in a long-term relationship **did you ever look at your single friends with envy** and wish you could have as much fun as them?

Because, as we all know, **the grass is always greener**, the chances are that now you are free the single life doesn't seem quite so glamorous. In fact, when you first separate life alone can seem downright scary. But fear not, that is where the fun really begins...

Making the most of SINGLEDOM

First of all, remember that **it's different for everyone.**

Spend a bit of time getting reacquainted with who you are. Try making a long **list of all the things that make you happy,** and make sure that you do at least one of them every day.

Stay in touch with your friends: keep all your lines of communication open and get out and about.

Don't rush into looking for someone new: most people can smell desperation a mile off, and it isn't attractive.

How to be SUCCESSFULLY single

1 **DON'T BE A REBOUND BABE**

Most women's first instinct when they hit the single zone is to run a mile in the other direction, probably straight back into a relationship – any relationship. **Don't rebound into another relationship straight away, it seldom works.**

2 **STOP WORRYING**

When we are reeling from a cold, hard dumping, **the initial feeling we have is fear.** We worry whether anyone will ever find us attractive again, whether we will have sex again and whether we will ever find our 'true love' and be happy. The answer is 'yes' to all these questions!

So don't waste all of your time worrying about getting older and ending up alone – it's not going to happen.

3 **FEEL THE FREEDOM**

You can eat what you like and when you like. Singletons can spend time with whomever they choose without having to 'check in' or ask for permission. **They can go out whenever they want to, or stay in when they don't feel like it.**

4 **BE SELFISH**

When single, if you don't have children, you can be totally focused and selfish and not feel guilty about it. **You can concentrate 100% on what it is that you want from life.** Where do you want to live? What colour do you want your living room to be? What sort of car do you want? Where do you want to go on holiday?

You can take up a language, hobbies or sports to meet new people and learn new things – **without having to run it by anyone else.**

5 ACHIEVE **THINGS**

This is the time to **try something you have always wanted to do** – especially if it was something your partner didn't want you to do.

Or you can **use** this time to **get in shape both mentally and physically.** Without having someone else in your life you have to get approval from, you can set some personal goals with complete freedom. As part of a couple, you really don't have that luxury because there is always someone else to consider.

6 REDISCOVER **YOUR FRIENDS**

You can now **spend time with the friends or family** that perhaps you have been neglecting. Better still, you no longer have to spend time with his friends and family, who you may not have liked anyway!

7 FIND **YOU**

All of us, when we become part of a couple, lose sight of who we really are. Somewhere along the way our identity can get lost in the merger with someone else – it's inevitable, especially in a long-term relationship. **Spend time finding out exactly what makes you tick.**

8 BE **SMUG**

When paired-off friends are moaning to you about their relationship, you can be thankful **you don't have to endure those sorts of problems any more** – for now anyway. . .

Single DOS and DON'TS

SHOULD I STAY IN TOUCH WITH MY EX?

It's the old cliché: **'I'd like us to stay friends'.** But do we mean it and will it work?

Yes: If kids are involved of course you'll be seeing each other again. In some cases, often after long-term relationships, there is so much history between you that you couldn't ever close the doors on each other anyway.

If you enjoy each other's company, why not stay friends? **If the sole reason for breaking up is that the love has gone, that doesn't mean the friendship has faded.** Tell others if you are remaining amicable, and tell each other when you are going to group gatherings of mutual friends.

No: Often the 'dumper' uses this line to soften the blow, knowing full well they won't be calling round for coffee. If you are the dumper, and your ex keeps ringing, you may actually have to be honest. If you were dumped, and they aren't returning your calls, get the message. **Friendship is a two-way thing and if only one of you is doing the running, it's not worth it.**

Staying in touch with your ex can also **make it hard to move on and rebuild your life.** You may decide to take a short break from each other so that you can get used to being apart and start to get your life in order before striking up a friendship. However, **you may decide it is better to have the good memories**, rather than get mad at each other through the difficulties of trying to be friends, and in these cases a clean break is necessary.

Finding Mr Right

Instead of sitting back and waiting for fate to bring him to your doorstep, take charge of the situation. You may have to make compromises that didn't seem so difficult when you were younger and more flexible. Learn from your mistakes and be realistic – there is no perfect Mr Right, but there are plenty of great men with whom you can have a long-lasting relationship.

First, you have to be ready, not just willing. This means being happy in your skin, confident and independent. You can't be looking for a man to be that last piece of the jigsaw puzzle. **Happiness comes from inside** – a good relationship should just be the icing on the cake. Plus, **being confident is sexy.**

Next, you need to be available – you can't be looking for Mr Replacement. **If you're not over your last relationship you will need to deal with those feelings first**. You always get an inaccurate view when you compare one man to another. Everyone is different and they have their own strengths and weaknesses.

Work out what YOU WANT

Make a list of qualities your Mr Right should have and a list of weaknesses you won't be able to tolerate. Then decide which qualities and weaknesses you will or will not compromise on. While attractiveness may seem important right now, realize that looks fade with time. **It is better to focus on quality of life** – things such as a positive attitude or a sense of humour. Your list should include what is important to you in a man, and what will make you happy.

EVALUATE your past

The next thing that you need to do is **list the characteristics of past lovers and ex-husbands.** What attracted you to them in the first place? How many of their traits match your list of needs? If there is little correlation between what you needed and what you got, see how all the men in your life were similar. If essential qualities for you are 'kind', 'considerate', and 'good-natured', yet you pick men who lack these qualities, but are either 'sexy', 'good-looking', or 'good in bed', realize the conflict that exists and be aware of it next time you meet someone.

Don't settle for less than your expectations just to be in a relationship. Knowing what you want before you start looking for love helps separate the good from the not-so-good, and allows you to find someone truly compatible for a possible lasting love.

SEX WITH YOUR EX

You may build bridges and become mates again, but once you get close **you may find yourselves back in lust**, and maybe back in love. However, if you feel your ex is only remaining in your life because they want you back, you will have to bring the topic up and stress that it's not going to happen. If you want them back too, think carefully before running back, **remember why you left in the first place.**

The MAN PLAN

Now you are ready to search. **Start by looking close to you**. Are there any colleagues or business associates you find attractive? Many women meet their future partners at work, which often means you will have similar backgrounds and have developed a friendship already. The following are good man-hunting activities. . .

SPEED IS OF THE ESSENCE

One evening, one date? That's so last year! Instead, **have 15 four-minute dates** and widen your options. There are dozens of speed-dating companies who organize evenings where you drink, chat and see who takes your fancy. So take a friend for support, a pencil to tick your sheet with, and who knows, you may just find a diamond in the rough.

LET YOUR FINGERS DO THE TALKING

Sign up to a reputable online dating agency and, **at the click of a mouse, watch the dates flood in.** It's great for those who work long hours, are shy or think it's just too difficult to meet people in the hectic twenty-first century.

If you are meeting someone for a date, always tell a friend or relative where you are going, who you are meeting, and when you will be back.

A MEETING OF MINDS

Enrol at an evening class and you're already guaranteed to have something in common. Whether your passion is for astronomy or bird watching, it can be the little things that bring people together.

MAN'S BEST FRIEND

Get a dog and when walking him, do some talent-spotting. **Pick strategic routes that take you past local eye-candy** in action, such as football grounds, tennis courts and so on. Watch out for sexy joggers and cyclists, too.

HEAD TO THE CHAPEL

There's no occasion on earth guaranteed to make you feel more warm and fuzzy than a wedding. So soak up all that love, **get yourself in prime position for catching the bouquet** and you could find yourself with a new man.

Marriage Survival Tips

Marriage should be an equal partnership where both parties can flourish, but this is often not the case – or at least not how it is all the time. Every marriage has its hurdles, but recognizing the danger signs as well as the dynamics that actually brought you together in the first place can go a long way toward turning your marriage into a good one throughout your life.

Are you in a CHILD-CHILD, PARENT-CHILD or BROTHER-SISTER partnership?

According to psychologists there are three distinct types of marriages. Although these categories may seem limiting, they can reveal quite a lot about how your marriage works.

In the child-child model, both parties are playing at being married and neither have matured enough to handle the more difficult aspects of marriage. This partnership is usually fun and lively, but volatile. If they manage to grow up together, and have sufficient money to enjoy life, this type of marriage can be a long one.

In the parent-child, one partner is the controlling parent and the other acquiesces. This can work well for a while, particularly if there is an age gap, but trouble starts when the child, almost inevitably, wants to grow up.

The brother-sister relationship is close and comforting. People tend to like people like themselves and this is true here. They usually share similar backgrounds and value systems. Unfortunately the erotic element, weak anyway, can become nonexistent. Because they have a strong comfort level together this relationship can last if it survives extramarital affairs.

12 TIPS for a GOOD MARRIAGE

1 **Watch what you say** – it can't be unsaid. Look out for words like 'You should have. . .' You don't. . .' and ' You never. . .' Substitute sentence structures like 'I would love it if. . .'

2 **Communicate, don't criticize.** Don't confront him, but bring up problems gently and calmly. Pause after you ask a question to give him time to respond without answering for him. If necessary, don't say anything at all until he answers, no matter how many minutes elapse.

3 **Don't go over old ground.** Recognize the triggers that each of you have that tip a conversation into argument. Old hurts are always there under the surface – resist bringing them into new conversations.

4 **Sort out your money problems.** Finances are the number-one trigger for arguments, so get them under control. Decide together how and when you will spend your money and your partnership will be in sync rather than resentful. Try to keep personal influences outside of money talk; the last thing you want to do is to discuss how 'he' isn't earning enough or 'she' spends too much money on shoes.

5 **Accept influence** from your partner. Instead of feeling like you're 'giving in' or being 'henpecked' into doing what your partner wants, accept that you are a couple and you each have equal weight. Research shows that women already are well practised at giving in to their husband's needs, but you will only have a true partnership when he can do this, too.

6 **End and repair arguments.** Find a way to exit arguments – with humour, compliments or signs of appreciation. If nothing works, agree to have a quiet break so you can calm down.

7 **Don't expect him to be a mind-reader:** just because you're married to him doesn't mean he knows what you want and when. Men tend to think, if she wants me to know she'll tell me, whereas women think, if he loves me he'll do it without me asking. You can see the problem.

8 **Keep it positive.** The happiest marriages are those where both couples have positive outlooks, so make sure this is reflected in the words you use to each other. Try to work on any negative thinking patterns you may have.

9 **Lower your tolerance** to hurtful comments. If you expect a high standard of behaviour from the start of a relationship – even simple politeness – you will be less likely to indulge in very poor behaviour and attitudes toward each other.

10 **Stay on the same team.** This is especially important when you have children as they need to see that you are together on issues important to them. At the same time, it is beneficial if they see you argue and resolve the problem – it will help them learn the same skills.

11 **Act like a couple.** The more you do together, the better your partnership will be. That's not to say that you need to give up rock climbing if your partner hates it, but keep an eye on how many things you do separately or the time you don't spend in each other's company.

12 **Trust is the cornerstone of a good marriage** – this can't be underestimated. When trust is broken we no longer feel safe. If there is something you feel you can't tell your partner, truly examine why – what are your fears and what do they reveal?

Marital Minefields

Is a kiss *really* being unfaithful?

A kiss is just a kiss? On the face of it, yes –
but you have to look at **what that kiss really means.**

If it's perfunctory, non-passionate and simply courteous then of course
it's not a problem. If it's a statement of affection from friend to friend then,
even if it's a smacker under the mistletoe, it's innocent. But where you get
into deep water is **when a kiss means more than courtesy or friendship**.
So if you know for sure that you are attracted to the person you're kissing,
then you're making a statement by going ahead. What are you saying by
this? What are you telling him? And what are you telling your partner?

Defining INFIDELITY

There are couples who have open relationships and are quite happy with their
situation. But here is where honesty comes into it. **Open relationships are
based on knowledge; infidelity is founded on lies and deceit.** The two basic
forms of infidelity are emotional and physical.

EMOTIONAL CHEATING ranges from knowingly dating someone else
behind your man's back or getting into a situation where you are so
emotionally close to someone that you fall in love with them. **Emotional
cheating is seen as less calculated** than physical cheating, but it is just as
deliberate in the sense that you often have to let yourself go before you
can fall for someone else.

PHYSICAL CHEATING means just that – **kissing, sexual petting, oral sex or
the ultimate, full-blown sex.** Most people in relationships define early on
what they would construe as cheating, with some including dirty dancing
with someone else as cheating; and others who do not view kissing another
person as a betrayal. Again, it goes back to individual values.

To TELL or NOT to tell?

Men are more likely to end a relationship when they discover infidelity. In other words, if you really want to save your relationship and are absolutely, 100 per cent certain that this will never happen again, then **sometimes it is best not to tell.**

Telling eases no one's conscience but your own and if your man is not the forgiving type, then you can **kiss him goodbye forever.**

Of course, in both situations, **it requires a lot of soul-searching on your part.**

Infidelity is a painful experience, especially for the person being cheated on. Finding out the root of your unfaithfulness is a good start, and this often **stems from being unhappy** with some part of your life, but not knowing what it is. The best advice is: don't do it in the first place. If there's a problem with your relationship, talk to your partner, and if this doesn't resolve things, it may be time to move on.

If you want to pursue another relationship **it will save a lot of deceit and hurt if you are single.**

Are you likely TO STRAY?

Take the following quiz to see if you are ripe for an affair. The more questions you answer yes to, the stronger the likelihood.

Do you feel:
- Your partner doesn't cuddle you as much as you would like?
- You'd like to have sex more than you do?
- Unappreciated by your partner?
- You'd prefer your partner to have a better paid or higher status job than he has?
- Your partner should listen to you more?
- Resentful your partner has had an affair?
- Your partner should pay you more attention?
- Disappointed or disillusioned in your relationship?

Why are YOU cheating?
THERE IS A REASON

There are **four main reasons** people have affairs –
here's how to address them.

FEELING UNLOVED

Often women are unfaithful because they want more physical affection
or emotional attention than they are getting from their current partner.

How to fix it

You need to talk this through with your man as soon as possible.
Be honest about your needs and why he's not meeting them,
then there's a good chance you can **nip the problem in the bud**
and avoid straying.

LACK OF SEX

Wanting more, or better, sex is another major factor
when it comes to having an affair.

How to fix it

Have you ever told your partner what you want in bed?
If not, now is the time to be honest, however difficult you
find it. If sex has become a serious problem it's well worth
talking to a relationship counsellor together so you can
get things back on track without either of you feeling the
need to look elsewhere.

DISILLUSIONMENT

Feeling that your partner isn't all you thought they were is another key affair trigger. Research shows that **women often have affairs with men who are more successful** or better paid than their current partner. And many women who have affairs do so only after their partners have already been unfaithful.

How to fix it

This is a tricky one, but it's important to remember all the reasons why you were attracted to your partner in the first place. And if that attraction really isn't there any more, and cannot be re-ignited, it is fairer to end the relationship rather than start an affair.

WANTING AN ESCAPE ROUTE

Sometimes we look for an affair to get us out of a relationship we have grown out of. **We just need a catalyst** to give us the confidence to end things once and for all.

How to fix it

Obviously it is far fairer – to you and your partner – if you can find the strength to end the relationship before you get as far as straying. If you're driven by a fear of being on your own that is something you need to address by yourself.

How to SPOT if he might be CHEATING

Is your partner...

★ Neglecting you?
★ No longer communicating with you?
★ Spending a lot of time away in unspecified locations?
★ Being generally evasive?

Look for changes that seem strange to you. Ironically, when someone is having an affair, their relationship can seem to take a turn for the better. Impromptu bunches of flowers or an improved sex life can both be signs of an affair. Often this is because your partner is enjoying a new lease of life, thanks to their liaison.

What to do if YOU'RE SURE he's having an AFFAIR

If you really believe your partner is having an affair, **you have to confront him with the evidence.** It's possible to try to ignore what you suspect, but it's very difficult to maintain a relationship, let alone your sanity, when you keep such feelings to yourself.

Broach the subject gently, even though your feelings may be running high – because if your partner is having an affair, this will make him clam up immediately – and if he isn't, he'll be angry, disappointed and offended.

If, on the other hand, your suspicions are confirmed and he is having an affair, **you have two choices of what to do next.**

LEAVE

The simplest choice. Refusing to take him back on any terms is certainly how you will feel initially, but how serious this desire to leave is will depend on the length of the affair; whether it was love or a one-night stand; and how many lies he told you to pursue it. If you feel you've been taken for a fool, and he's shown no respect for your feelings, **leaving may be the only sensible option.**

It will, however, turn your life upside down, physically, emotionally and financially, and when the smoke clears, **you could be left regretting your haste**, so make sure it's what you really want.

STAY

Choosing to remain with your partner after discovering infidelity is much harder. You know that sex is going to be impossible for months to come, because you can't stop thinking about him with her. **There is also the very real danger that your anger and resentment at his betrayal will destroy your relationship anyway.** But coping with the knowledge that it happened, and forgiving him, is certainly the biggest challenge your relationship will ever face.

The Temptation of Toy Boys – Is Age Really Just a Number?

We've become used to seeing red-carpet couples flying in the face of convention when it comes to modern age-gap relationships. But it seems **they represent a steadily increasing trend.**

According to the Office of National Statistics over 50 per cent of all couples who married in England and Wales in 2003 were outside the so-called 'normal' five-year age gap.

And, of course, no official statistics exist for couples in long-term relationships outside marriage, but we have to assume that the number of them is higher still.

As men and women's roles within society have become more equal, our ideas of what makes a perfect mate have evolved. **A man and woman of the same age, with the standard 2.4 children combination, is no longer the only model of a successful relationship.** We have come to realize that matching personalities, not ages, is far more important when it comes to making love work.

Women at 30, 40 and even 50 are healthier, fitter and younger-looking than ever, which means that a few years here or there mean far less physically than they did even a decade ago. First and foremost, the issue is much less whether there's an age gap, or how wide such a gap might be, than what makes a relationship work.

All of which may go to explain **the rise of the toy boy** – a phenomenon so common it rarely raises an eyebrow these days.

One of the best things about a younger guy is his enthusiasm – for life and you. Older men can seem cynical and suspicious, armed to the hilt with a lifetime of relationship baggage and wary of what, or who, might come next. Plus having a toy boy can restore your sense of fun.

But what about the future? Your love may be great right now, but what about five, ten or even 20 years down the line? **What we want from life evolves as our experience changes.**

Will a couple who are at such different life stages be able to work through this, or will their wildly different needs eventually end up driving them apart?

Types of Men to Avoid at All Costs

There are **several kinds of guys** you should steer clear of while on the singles' scene. It will save you time and heartache in the long run.

Here are some of the worst ones.

THE BAD BOY

Characteristics: Charming and fun-loving, he can also be cruel. One minute you're the only woman who understands him, the next his friends or his work come first, and you'd better back off if you want to keep him.

Why you'll be tempted: When bad boys are good, they're very, very good. They know how to lavish love and affection on a woman, making her feel cherished.

Why you should run: It won't last. No matter how much you think you'll be able to change him, you won't. Bad boys get bored quickly.

Danger sign: He stands you up to go out with his mates.

THE MUMMY'S BOY

Characteristics: Sweet, but soft, he may have a bit of a belly from all those home-cooked meals. Worse still, he may actually still live at home with his mummy and daddy.

Why you'll be tempted: He'll watch chick flicks with you.

Why you should run: He's actually already seen them all with his mum.

Danger sign: He tells you he thinks his mother will love you and tries to get you to meet her after just one date.

THE GYM FANATIC

Characteristics: Hunky, tough, always up for a spontaneous game of football, and dressed in tracksuit and trainers.

Why you'll be tempted: Those fantastic muscles.

Why you should run: All the hours he spends at the gym bulking up those muscles, not to mention the hours spent gazing at his reflection in the mirror.

Danger sign: He watches sports on TV constantly and can't be distracted by any of your sexual advances.

MR ULTRA-COOL

Characteristics: Well-dressed and confident, he knows the latest fashion trends even better than you do, which is worrying.

Why you'll be tempted: Other women will stop to stare and drool with jealousy when he's on your arm.

Why you should run: His wardrobe will make yours look poor by comparison and you'll always be worried about keeping up with him.

THE SMOOTHIE

Characteristics: Whether he's traditionally handsome or a diamond in the rough, there's just something about this guy that makes you swoon. And he treats women like gold because he loves them – all of them – so much.

Why you'll be tempted: He knows how to compliment, woo and thrill you through and through.

Why you should run: He uses the same routine on every woman he meets.

Danger sign: He forgets your name while you're in bed.

THE WORKAHOLIC

Characteristics: High-profile businessman who is smart, ambitious, impeccably dressed and completely unavailable.

Why you'll be tempted: He's dapper, charming and successful. What's not to love?

Why you should run: See the 'completely unavailable' part above.

Danger sign: He has to check his diary before agreeing to a date – even after you've been seeing each other for six months.

THE STALKER

Characteristics: Sweet, romantic but not very sexy. He loves planning outings and thinks you are by far the most important thing in his life – ever.

Why you'll be tempted: He's the sensitive guy who everyone says just needs a chance, plus he'll do anything for you.

Why you should run: He really will do anything for you, which can be very scary.

Danger sign: He tells you he wants to spend more time with you – after three dates.

Love Potential Checklist

DON'T see him again if. . .

1 **You're looking for a serious relationship** and he says he never wants to settle down.

2 **He has debt problems –** make it easy for yourself by only dating men who are financially stable.

3 **He can't keep a job.** You want someone responsible you can count on in your life.

4 **He shows signs of a bad temper.**

5 **He can't keep his eyes off members of the opposite sex.** You want to be the only one in your man's life.

6 **He sounds bitter** about love or life in general.

7 **His background, values and religious beliefs are totally opposite to yours.** It might seem exciting and challenging at the beginning, but it's not likely to work in the long-run.

8 **He comes across as always wanting to steal the show,** no matter what. It might be fun at the beginning, but you don't want to live life in someone's shadow.

Is It Time to Move On?

Treading water in a so-so relationship can be just as unhealthy as staying in a downright bad one. Take the following quiz to **find out what state your relationship is in** – and whether it's worth saving.

1 How often do you argue with your man?

a) Most days.
b) Quite often.
c) From time to time.
d) Almost never.

2 Which statement best describes how you pick up the pieces and get back to normal after a row?

a) We usually end up laughing and then forgetting about it.
b) We sit and thrash things out, but then move on quite quickly.
c) We often go to bed on a row, but one of us usually says sorry in the morning and everything's OK again.
d) It can take days before we speak to each other again.

3 What would you say causes the majority of the rows in your relationship?

a) Sex.
b) Not spending enough time together.
c) Money.
d) Differing views on life.

4 Which of the following areas causes you the most stress in your life?

a) Your relationship with your partner.
b) Work.
c) I don't tend to get stressed.
d) Trying to juggle everything.

5 Does your partner make you feel confident about yourself and emotionally secure?

a) Always.
b) Usually.
c) Rarely.
d) Never.

6 Do you trust your partner to be faithful?

a) Yes – he'd never stray.
b) Everyone's human, but I don't think he would be unfaithful.
c) Not when things are going badly between us.
d) No, I strongly suspect he's had affairs or at least seriously thought about it.

7 What's your first reaction to the thought of splitting up with your partner?

a) There are times when I think about splitting up, but always end up staying.
b) I'd be devastated, but I would just have to pull myself together and move on.
c) I'd feel relieved in many ways.
d) I can't imagine life without him.

8 How would you describe your sex life?

a) Pretty good most of the time.
b) Pretty boring these days.
c) Fantastic.
d) Non-existent.

9 If you're feeling stressed after a hard day at work does seeing and talking to your partner make you feel better?

a) Sometimes, but talking to a close friend is usually more helpful.
b) I might be grumpy with him to start with, but he'll often do something sweet that cheers me up.
c) Always – the thought of him is what gets me through the day.
d) No, we usually end up rowing and I feel worse.

10 In your opinion, how happy is your relationship?

a) Very.
b) Pretty good most of the time.
c) Not very happy these days.
d) It's happy about 50 per cent of the time.

WORK OUT YOUR RELATIONSHIP'S HEALTH RATING

Match your answers to the corresponding shapes and tot up your total. If you have the same number of two shapes, you're probably a mixture, so read each summary that applies to you.

	a)	b)	c)	d)
1	▲	●	■	★
2	★	●	■	▲
3	■	★	●	▲
4	▲	■	★	●
5	★	●	■	▲
6	★	●	■	▲
7	■	●	▲	★
8	●	■	★	▲
9	■	●	★	▲
10	★	●	▲	■

THE DIAGNOSIS:

★ Mostly stars
TOO HEALTHY FOR YOUR OWN GOOD?

Couples that never argue or express different views may be setting themselves up for a fall. Many people associate a low number of rows with the 'perfect relationship', but this isn't necessarily the case. **One of the key ways in which relationships grow is by learning to reconcile your differences.** If you find yourself always agreeing with your partner and fitting in with what they want for a peaceful life, there's a danger frustration and resentment will build up, which is bad for your relationship.

WHAT YOU CAN DO:

Don't be afraid to be your own person a bit more. **Being loved-up is fantastic, but it also makes you very self-absorbed.** The difficulty comes when you make changes that cost you in terms of your relationships with others, or when you make damaging work or health sacrifices. Be certain any changes you or your partner make are positive ones that benefit you both.

Mostly circles
A CLEAN BILL OF HEALTH

An enviable state to be in – a recent US study found that **couples who had sex at least three times a week actually felt and looked ten years younger!** Being in a stable relationship also means you have a safe haven to go to, regardless of what problems the outside world throws at you. Such mutual support will boost both your confidence and well being.

WHAT YOU CAN DO:

Keep up the good work, but a word of caution – if you've not been together for long, you may still be experiencing the 'high' of falling in love. **Infatuation makes the brain release feel-good chemicals called phenylethylamines (PEAs) that make everything thing seem rosy.** However, two years is the maximum time the body can continuously produce PEAs, after which normality sets in and you may find you have to work a bit harder to keep the spark alive.

Try organizing surprise dinners or sending each other sexy text messages. Anything that stops you taking each other for granted and shows your partner you still think they're worth making an effort for.

Mostly Squares

LOOKING A BIT PEAKY

A recent report by Brigham Young University in the US found that **OK, but not great, relationships can be worse than bad ones.** Being in a constant state of uncertainty about whether to continue or not in a relationship can cause feelings of anxiety, insecurity and even raise blood pressure. It can also create feelings of guilt, if you can't pinpoint why you feel unhappy. This is often the time when people have, or contemplate, affairs.

WHAT YOU CAN DO:

Don't focus on the doom and gloom of the situation. Take this as an opportunity to do some soul-searching and to rediscover all the reasons why you got together in the first place. **Try to rekindle feelings of intimacy.** Being more touchy-feely – in a non-sexual way – can work wonders.

And if you both have demanding careers, it's important to make time for each other and not fall into a 'I'm more stressed than you are' competition. Often by working longer hours and taking on more commitments we're really trying to avoid something at home, so think carefully whether this is the case, then **confront the issue and work out how you can both prioritize your time better.**

Mostly triangles
CALL IN THE **CRASH TEAM...**

Constantly arguing and feeling miserable in a relationship will have **a huge impact on both of you.** Even in the twenty-first century, women still tend to take on the role of carer in a relationship. This can mean juggling a demanding career, with all the household tasks and childcare, resulting in stress, sleep deprivation and depression. Problems can also arise if one partner suddenly becomes more successful, disturbing the delicate balance of power that existed when you first met.

WHAT YOU CAN DO:

It's make or break time and you have to **decide whether the relationship is worth saving.** If you've invested a lot in the relationship and children are involved make sure, before leaving, that the relationship can't be improved to a state where it's genuinely acceptable to both of you. This may mean getting professional help.

Even if there are no compelling reasons to stay together, it's a good idea to **try and understand why the relationship hasn't worked** – to stop you making the same mistakes next time.

Troubles in Paradise: How to Ride Out the Storm

If you notice that you're not getting on as usual, there are definite steps you can take to turn things around. The first hurdle, always, is recognizing you're in trouble in

the first place. Try to identify if it's a short-term or long-term problem. Lingering friction or resentment from a previous argument can last for days; alternatively if **the gulf between you seems to grow wider** and impacts on social events and activities you do together, it may be time for a heart-to-heart.

Tackling TROUBLESPOTS

All marriages hit crisis point occasionally. The tips below can
help you rescue your relationship from the brink of disaster,
or at worst identify when the problem is big enough that you
may need outside help for the partnership to survive.

IF HE WALKS AWAY

Give him time to sulk and come back to you with any grievances or to
discuss what's on his mind. If he wants to end things, it rarely helps to beg or
plead him to stay. Keep your dignity. You cannot control him, only yourself,
and the relationship requires both people to agree to make it work.

AVOID THE BLAME GAME

Look at both sides of the problem and try to put yourself in his place –
you are both accountable for the marriage, and any failure is a mutual one.
You might realize that you've been too busy with children or career plans
to pay enough attention to him, or you may have neglected to include him
in decisions, in which case he may be feeling marginalized and useless.

BE CAREFUL WHO YOU CONFIDE IN

You need to be communicating with him, not his mother or your
sister. Giving too much information to friends or other family
members may backfire on you and can cause further tension.

DO RATHER THAN SAY

Small acts of kindness can make him feel important and
loved when things have been tense and troubled in a way
that no amount of words will ever do.

FOCUS ON THINGS THAT BRING YOU CLOSER

Rewinning your marriage is a complex, difficult task but start
with goals about what you want to improve. Whatever strategy
you employ for saving your marriage or getting through the
tough spot, make sure your approach is designed to bring you
two closer together. Any tactic that has negative repercussions
should be avoided at all costs.

When Splitting Up is the Only Option

Deciding to break up with a long-term partner or get divorced from a spouse is a big decision. You should understand that **you aren't a bad person just because things didn't work.**

Once a divorce has been set in motion, people often feel a brief sense of relief. This is usually replaced by anxiety at the prospect of all the things still left to do before life gets back on an even keel. **Here's how to cope.**

Do:

- Allow yourself to mourn.
- Get appropriate legal help.
- Keep a careful watch on your physical and emotional health, and get help from a counsellor if necessary.
- Talk to supportive friends and relatives.
- Get organized and deal with practical issues, such as your finances.
- Take one day at a time and believe that things will change for the better.

Don't:

- Expect too much of yourself.
- Get involved in small wranglings over possessions.
- Rush into new relationships in an attempt to make yourself feel better.
- Hang on to feelings of anger because this will prevent you moving on.

The Moving On Masterplan

STAGE ONE

1 Don't see him
If he has to come to your place, arrange for someone else to be there. Ban him from dropping in casually and ask him to remove the rest of his stuff from the house as soon as possible.

2 Don't contact him
No more 'how are you getting on?' emails or 'I've just found that shirt of yours' phone calls. Forget about excuses to get in touch. It just keeps you hanging in there and hoping. If he's contacting you, ask him not to. Of course, if you have children this will not be possible, but limit your communication to necessary arrangements and information about the children.

3 Talk about him less
Going over every detail of what happened with friends may feel comforting initially, but after a few weeks it's time to stop. Friends get bored and you get stuck. So be very selective about what you say and the people you say it to and start talking about other things.

4 Stop beating yourself up
So you weren't perfect. Well neither was he. You both did your best to make it work and it didn't. Put it down to experience and forget about blaming him or yourself. Blaming anyone hurts only you and holds you back from recovery.

5 Tell yourself you're over it
Imagine a date a few weeks away when instead of feeling awful you'll wake up and know you're over it. The sun will come out, gorgeous men will seem to be on every street corner and you'll feel like going out and living life again.

Why wait? Make that day come more quickly. Feel the excitement of knowing you did it, you survived and life is good again. Now hang on to that feeling.

STAGE TWO

1 *Know you're gorgeous*

One of the hardest things about breaking up is that your self-esteem takes a tumble and you have to rebuild it step by step. Feeling attractive is vital, and anyone can do it. Tell yourself you're sexy, charismatic, bright and desirable – and listen to friends who think you are, too. Pamper yourself, even if you don't feel like it and don't think it will make a difference. Before you know it, you'll be feeling like a fully-fledged sex kitten again.

2 *Become an accomplished flirt*

It is really important now to meet lots of people – men and women – and talk, smile, flirt, take an interest and laugh with them. Life as part of a couple often limits contact with other people. Now it's time to get really sociable.

Don't know how to meet people? This is an excuse to hide behind. If you want to meet people, you will. Make a list, right now, of all the ways you could do this. Join an evening class you've always wanted to take, such as Italian. Try something physically demanding like training for a marathon or arrange a get-together with old friends.

3 *Don't rush into dating*

Tempting though it might be, try not to jump into a new relationship too hastily. The rule tends to be that if you rush in fast, it will end fast too. So go slowly. If you fancy someone, great, but hold back for a while and remember that this new you is in charge and needn't hurry.

Back on the Scene

Ten ways to AVOID dating disaster

There is (love) life after divorce – here's how to make a smooth transition **from downbeat divorcee to fun and flirty dater.**

1   Wait until the divorce papers are through!
Having romantic encounters during the last stages of separation can have disastrous effects on the divorce – and your emotions. Not only will it save you some explanations in court, it will also speed up the process and help set you free faster.

2   Wash him right out your hair.
Now that you're officially divorced, single and ready to start dating, you need to achieve proper closure. If you still talk to your ex regularly – stop. If you have some of his things at your home, post them back. It's impossible to let go and hold on at the same time.

3   Turn your bedroom into a boudoir.
This means throwing away – or at the very least storing – all those little keepsakes and presents he gave you and any old photographs. Buy a new set of luxurious, sexy bed-linen and give the walls a fresh coat of paint.

4   Don't let bitterness steer you away from nice men.
Resist the temptation to find somebody who's the exact opposite to your ex. Remember, there were a lot of things about him that were appealing and attractive when you first met.

5   Make a love and lust list.
Write down exactly what you're looking for in a partner. It will help you see in black and white exactly what you want – and some things may come as a surprise.

6 Have fun.
If you were married for a long time it can be tempting to jump straight into something serious. But before you do, ask yourself, is it simply because you want to feel secure again? Dating lots of different types of men is a good way of finding out what your options are – and helps you realize that you DO have options.

7 Don't be scary.
Be very careful not to engage in premature 'couple' behaviour or excessive phone ringing after two dates just because it's what you know best. You don't want to ruin something good by overwhelming him before you've even got to know each other.

8 Experiment.
Approach the dating scene with an open mind. Don't be obsessed with finding Mr Right. Meeting Mr Right Now can be just as good!

9 Be honest with yourself.
You'll know by the second or third date whether you're vaguely interested in a guy. If you're dreading seeing him again, be brave enough to say no.

10 Flirt 'til it hurts.
It's fun, sexy and playful and the oldest form of human contact and connection. It's about charming someone and letting yourself be charmed. Best of all it doesn't have to mean anything serious – unless you want it to, that is...

How to Play the Dating Game

When you begin dating **after a few years out of the game it can be pretty scary**. It can seem like a whole other world, with its own unspoken rules and codes that can easily be broken without you even realizing.

What is vital to remember is that while there will always be men who try their luck, dating should be about **two people coming together to see whether they are compatible** and then, if they want to, moving towards forming a relationship.

Here are a few bits of **important dating etiquette** to help things go smoothly.

- **Dating should always be fun** and it is as much your responsibility as your date's to make sure it is. When you are dating ensure that you do everything you can to make the meeting enjoyable.
- **Eye contact is crucial** when dating so provide as much attention as possible to your date. They should feel that they are the only person in the room.
- **You should always turn up for a date** unless you have given plenty of time for it to be cancelled. Standing someone up is not acceptable adult behaviour.
- **Drinking copious amounts on dates is not a good idea** – ever. One or two drinks to get the conversation flowing between you is fine.
- **Try not to be too opinionated** and avoid discussions on politics and religion in the early stages.
- **Be a good listener** and don't talk your date to death.
- **Never ever discuss your ex-boyfriends** or how many people you have slept with on a first date.

Dating again

Although it may be obvious that you should avoid too-low tops and too-high hemlines, as well as drinking too much and showing pictures of your kids or former partner, there are other subtler no-nos that will help you avoid dating failures. Keeping a light, open and positive approach, and asking questions about the other person, is always a good start.

How to Break Your Bad Dating Habits

When it comes to men do you find yourself falling into the same trap time after time? The result being **you scare off the right person, or end up with the wrong one.** If so, it's time to break your bad dating habits once and for all.

SEX ON THE FIRST DATE

After first-date sex, nothing will be the same. If you even see each other again you won't get to know each other properly as you will have skipped too many stages. So if you like them and see a future in it, don't do it. If he really does turn out to be your soul mate **you've got the rest of your life to sleep with him** so don't be in such a hurry.

YOU ALWAYS GO FOR THE SAME TYPE

The problem with this pattern is that if this was the right type of person for you, you'd still be with one of them. **Good couples are those who are well matched in terms of personality, outlook on life and similarity of attitudes.** The chances are, by always going for a type, you will rarely have any of these things in common. Ask your friends if they think you go for one type of person, or adopt a particular role in your relationships that holds you back. This will give you an idea of the traps you fall into and you can work out ways to avoid them.

YOUR EVERY PORE
SHOUTS 'DESPERATE'

We all know that men can smell a woman who is desperate to settle down at any cost a mile off. And **once he picks up that scent he'll run as fast as humanly possible** in the opposite direction. Making an effort to find new interests, new friends and so on will stop you ending up with the only man you didn't manage to scare off. Always ask yourself: **'If I had endless time and choices, would I choose him?'** If the answer's no, finish it now.

YOU EXPECT TO MEET MR RIGHT IN A BAR

It's a sad fact that the older we get, the smaller the pool of eligible men gets, so you need to go out of your way to find them. This doesn't mean trawling as many clubs and pubs as you can find – **the men there are rarely looking for love.** Instead you need to change your routine: buy coffee somewhere different; try a new evening class; or take a different bus to work, and so on.

Of course, it's one thing seeing people and another talking to them. Try carrying a conversation-starting book that reflects aspects of your personality in the hope a like-minded man might notice it or, failing that, it will give you something to do so you don't look like you're aimlessly hanging around. Or, **if you spot someone you really like, bump into them 'accidentally' and spark up a conversation** – you've nothing to lose.

YOU FEEL THE NEED
TO DISCUSS YOUR EX

We've all gone through heartache in the past, but **tonight's date probably doesn't want to hear** about it in detail.

The danger in not letting go of your ex is that you create a perfect memory of him that no one will ever live up to. Take some time to **remind yourself of all his bad points and move on!**

Love Second Time Around

After a break-up it can seem like you'll never find love again. But then you do – and it feels amazing. But whether you're planning to get married or just move in together, **there are certain things you can do to make sure the relationship is for keeps** this time.

LEARN
FROM THE PAST

Make sure you learn the lessons that have come out of your old relationship. Think through how you met, how you chose to be with each other, how your love developed, and how you handled problems. **Think about what went wrong and why.** Once you know this, you'll be far better placed to make a second relationship work.

GET TO KNOW
YOUR NEW LOVE

It's particularly important to **really get to know the person you are committing to in a second relationship**, because of what both of you are bringing into the situation: more age, more experience, more history, and consequently more potential for problems.

Find out how he feels, thinks and what he wants out of life. Make sure you discuss not only your past relationships and what went wrong, but your early life and how this has shaped you into the person you are.

TROUBLEshooting for second marriages

Some problems crop up again and again. **Here are four of the most common problem spots**, and how you can handle them.

1 Sharing space

The older you are, the harder it is to move into someone else's life or have them move into yours. Be prepared to accommodate. Allow each of you to have 'private space' – if possible, your own room where you can have things your way.

Make sure you do things together, but also allow for time alone when you can both have the chance to do things independently of each other.

2 The ex-factor

It can be tricky if an ex is still part of your partner's life. The secret is to remember that you have split from your respective exes for very good reasons and have now chosen to be with each other. The ex, however difficult and awkward, is history. Put your jealousy to one side and concentrate on developing a united front. Make a deal with your partner about how you are going to handle your ex-partners.

3 Playing mum

Second marriages often come with a ready-made family, which can be hard to adapt to. The secret to avoiding difficulty is the same secret that underpins all strong relationships – communication. Talk about how you are going to handle your kids in terms of discipline, time and attention.

4 Repeating the past

If you find yourself slipping into the same rows and uncomfortable situations with your new love as you did with your old one, don't panic. It's not surprising – you are still the same person and will slip into the same patterns of behaviour. But the key thing to remember in all relationships is that it is possible to change – if you truly want to.

5 Expect the unexpected

Be prepared for things not going as you imagined. Keep in mind that there are many ways to suceed at a task and that your new partner will bring new challenges and new expectations. Keep communication lines open at all times.

6 Schedules and house rules

Stepfamilies have complicated lives to schedule. Try to liaise as much as possible with the ex-spouses so everyone is crystal clear about what is happening when. Lay down the law in your own home, but don't try to do the same in someone else's. You may rationalize that this is for their own good, but don't kid yourself.

7 The green-headed monster

Begin early to develop a relationship with any stepchildren but do not expect them to give you anything back. The child's primary bond is with their natural parents and it's in the interest of their survival instinct to guard this, so jealousy is common. Encourage your new partner has to spend enough time with his children.

8 Discuss money matters before you marry
Because your financial arrangements are certain to be complicated, with alimony or maintenance payments and children, make sure you are both aware of the score before you move in together. This includes cash-flow and investment as well as plans for your will.

9 Dealing with loss
Ongoing emotional upheavals for children and your partner will be natural – losing a wife and mother is not something you can 'get over' and there is a tendency to idealize the person. Be supportive but also watch out for your own feelings of resentment. Talk to a counsellor if you feel this could develop into a problem.

10 Half-sibling troubles
Relationships take time. Don't expect half-siblings to instantly like each other and don't be frightened of actual, intense dislike – this will usually pass with time. Any visiting siblings should have a space of their own in your home. Avoid favouring your own children, but also avoid overcompensating and favouring his children – treat all with respect and fairness.

CHAPTER

Fashion for the Fabulous

Your Ultimate Style Clinic

Just when you think you have your look all worked out, the **new season catches you offguard**. It might be the return of the miniskirt; a hot colour that suddenly dominates after years of neutrals; or an obsession with floaty frills, when you love the tomboy look.

But fashion addicts should take note: **women who have great style understand one thing – when to say no.** Knowing what will work, and what would look better on someone with another body or another life, is the key to fashion success.

What makes a boring basic for one woman can look like the height of cool on another; it can turn that charity shop bargain into a stunning and unique outfit for the woman who is clever enough to know it has her name on it. Looking stylish and cool is not about buying as many 'in fashion' items as possible and throwing them all together. **It's about knowing what to choose from the latest season and leaving the rest well alone.**

Here are **five ways** to make difficult trends work for you – without making you look like a desperate fashion victim.

1 Bright colours

It can be like coming back into the sunshine after years of wearing black, but a bright colour can also make you look like a clown. Absorb the colour gradually until you can be sure you are confident with it. Start with a scarf or some simple knitwear to brighten up your neutrals. Gradually, as you become sure of what colours work best for you, make bolder statements.

Stacked heels

Good shoes are essential. They hold the power to make or break an outfit. But it is worth remembering that not every shape will be flattering on you.

Chunky heels come in and out of fashion and are easier to balance on than a stiletto, but they can make thick legs look even wider. And beware of ankle straps – they shorten and thicken all but the thinnest leg. The most universally flattering shoe style is a pair of sexy high heels. They make your legs look longer and slimmer and can give you a great confidence boost. But stick to no higher than 3 cm (2 in) to make sure you don't totter.

Prints

An all-over print is actually a good way to disguise figure faults because it keeps the eye moving across the body, but choose smaller prints if you're trying to look slimmer or if you are short in stature. Large prints only look striking on tall, model-like figures.

Frills and ruffles

Excessive frills can seem too girly and fussy on grown-up women. And full-on frills should be avoided by anyone on the chubby side. But a pretty blouse with a hint of frill at the neckline and cuff eases up the most formal suits and makes trousers look glamorous. Frills and ruffles are also great if you have a boyish figure and want to create curves.

Miniskirts

The sad truth is, even if you have the most perfect pins in the world, you won't carry off very short skirts once you pass the age of 25. Be scrupulously honest with yourself! If you're still determined to go short, stick to a hem that just skims the tops of the knees.

Make FASHION FAUX PAS
a thing of the past

Even the most stylish of us make fashion mistakes from time to time. Here's a list of some of the worst and advice on how to avoid them.

YOUR CLOTHES ARE TOO TIGHT

We have all squeezed into a size smaller than we really are – it makes us feel slimmer to say 'I got into a small' when really a medium would have been more comfortable. However, **there is nothing guaranteed to make you look bigger than you really are than too-tight clothes.** Always wear your 'real' size.

YOUR CLOTHES ARE TOO LOOSE

Another common mistake is to wear baggy clothes to try and hide excess weight, but be warned: this simply adds even more pounds. Instead, **accentuate your positive points and show off your curves.** Fitted tops and trousers are far more flattering than over-sized tent-like dresses.

YOU ARE MIXING TOO MANY STYLES

Don't make the mistake of trying to satisfy everything that is currently in fashion with one outfit. **You will look like you are trying too hard.**

YOU HAVEN'T IRONED YOUR CLOTHES

What's the point of spending hours choosing the perfect outfit only to not iron it properly before you go out? **No clothes look good wrinkled** – no matter how expensive they are – so always keep a good steam iron handy. If you really hate ironing, **buy clothes made from fabrics that don't crumple as much.** If you are on holiday and have no iron, hang up clothes in the bathroom – the steam from the bath and shower will help the creases drop out.

THE WRONG ACCESSORIES

Top off your look with accessories that match your style. Choose the correct length necklace to suit the neckline of your top or dress. **Short chains and chokers tend to make your neck appear larger.** And never wear necklaces over the top of jumpers.

Tricks to Hide Your Body Flaws

Try these **easy cheats** to beat the four most common body shape dilemmas.

PEAR-shaped

Have your hips caused you years of tears when it comes to looking good? Here's how to minimize them.

Skirts: Fuller, below-the-knee skirts conceal wider hips. Avoid pencil skirts and opt for A-line styles and skirts with hemline details, which balance your shape.

Trousers: Sport fuller, wide-leg shapes. Avoid cropped trousers which make your legs look shorter.

Dresses: Nipped-in waists with fuller skirts can hide a multitude of sins! Try strapless shapes to draw the eye upward and away from your lower half.

Jackets: Stick to longer styles that camouflage the hip area.

Tops: Choose halterneck styles and boat necks, which create the illusion of broader shoulders to balance out bulk below.

Pot BELLY or Bulging Love HANDLES

Follow these simple tips to minimize a wide waistline.

Dresses: Look for styles that have gathered fabric to pull you in at the middle, and V-necks, which draw the eye upward.

Tops: Make sure they stop before the tummy to avoid them clinging to any bulges. Layered tops made from chiffon or silk help create the illusion of slimness.

Jackets: Choose well-cut, tailored jackets to create a slimmer waist.

Trousers: Go for trouser suits with a wide leg – the more lines and seams, the less attention will be paid to bulges around the belly.

Skirts: Choose full skirts rather than pencil shapes as they will be more forgiving of a big tummy.

Too SHORT

You can only add so many inches with high heels – try some of these tricks instead.

Trousers: Long, wide-leg trousers lengthen legs. Pinstripes are also great if you want to look taller.

Skirts: Short skirts will always add height. They don't have to be minis, just-above-the-knee lengths work too. Steer clear of long skirts at all costs, though.

Jackets: Keep them short and sweet. Longer jackets will make you seem smaller.

Dresses: Stick to dresses that are simple and classic in shape – avoid fussy details like ruffles and bows as they can make you look even shorter.

Tops: Look for tops that finish on the hips – any longer and they will drown your body frame.

Too BOYISH

Don't worry if your hourglass figure never did materialize – you can still cheat and add curves in all the right places.

Jackets: Try a bit of non-surgical nip and tuck. Tapered jackets will help accentuate busts and waistlines.

Skirts: Pair a full skirt with a long top and add a thin belt to help create a waist.

Tops: Corset-style tops will create a super-sexy shape, as will V-necks and scoop necks.

Dresses: Choose ones with a fitted waist for instant curves.

Trousers: Steer clear of wide-leg trousers as they simply emphasize your lack of curves. Instead, make the most of your slim thighs with close-fitting, straight-leg shapes.

What to Wear When

Knowing what to wear and when is the key to good style. To do this successfully, you need to **make your wardrobe work for you.** That means keeping it flexible and making sure you have something for every occasion.

Wearing the right clothes can help your career progress, while inappropriate outfits may mean you are passed over for promotion. They can attract the right sort of man, boost your self confidence and, most important of all, **send a strong message to the outside world about what type of woman you are**.

But sometimes the stresses and strains of **juggling a career and family means that fashion goes by the wayside,** and before you know it you find yourself putting the way you look way down on your list of priorities. But looking good is vital to your self-esteem and should never be dismissed as being vain or a waste of time.

Do a quick wardrobe maintenance check every few months to make sure that you **have clothes handy for every possible occasion.** Ask yourself what you would wear if you were invited to. . . a wedding this weekend. . . a party tonight. . . a job interview next week. . . or on a date tomorrow evening.

Now **head to your wardrobe and make sure you have a fail-safe outfit** for each of these occasions. If you don't, whatever is missing should be your next clothing investment. Do this regularly and you'll always have something handy to wear for last-minute invites.

Identify your favourite fashion style and try to modify it for every possible occasion. For example, if you are a jeans and boots girl, add a sparkly top for a night-time party, wear with a tailored jacket for work, slip on a halterneck and strappy sandals or wedges for a summer party or dress down with trainers (sneakers) and a classic T or hoodie for weekend casual.

Accessorize. Every outfit can benefit from being pulled together with interesting belts, brooches, bags, scarves or jewellery. **Stick to two coordinated accessories** and check the balance – bold minimalist shapes and colours can take oversized or opulent jewellery, but intricate necklines need a delicate approach.

Don't forget what you will be wearing on top of your outfit. The overall effect of many a stunning outfit has been spoiled by wearing the wrong outer garment. The reason pashminas are so loved is that they can go with anything from jeans to formal wear. Check both the length and the fabric weight are compatible with your outfit, as well as the style and colour.

Beat the morning RUSH HOUR

We've all been there. **Woken up late on a Monday morning** when there's a meeting, presentation or lunch date we wanted to look great for. Suddenly we're bolting out of bed and heading for the wardrobe in a mad panic.

What on earth can I wear?

Don't worry. The following wardrobe essentials will make sure you give off the message that you're organized, beautiful and in control, plus help you **pull your look together super quickly.**

A WELL-TAILORED JACKET

Always have one good, well-tailored jacket in your wardrobe. If it fits you well, you can **throw it on over anything,** and you'll look instantly polished.

When looking for a good cut, make sure the shoulder seams sit at the shoulder, not below, as this can look messy.

THE 'PERFECT' TOP

Fitted T-shirts and shirts in a wide variety of colours are **the staple of any versatile wardrobe.** For a great shape, choose fabrics with a hint of stretch but not too much – or they will cling to lumps and bumps. A classic tailored shirt will look great for work and can also be dressed down at weekends with jeans.

A SMART JUMPER

Invest in at least one, high-quality knit jumper. **Go for cashmere, it's always worth the extra money.** For one thing, it will last longer than your average sweater, plus it's far less likely to fade, pull or need ironing. For warmer weather, cashmere-cotton blends are perfect. In cooler climates, a heavier cashmere-wool blend can't be beaten.

A WRAP DRESS

Everyone should have at least one fabulous dress. Nothing is simpler. This classically chic wrap-front jersey is an impeccable choice because **it's flattering, feminine** and works everywhere, from the boardroom to your child's classroom. You can just slip it on and instantly you appear pulled together.

BAG AND SHOES THAT CORRESPOND

They don't have to match exactly – in fact this can seem quite dated – but **look for corresponding touches.** If you're wearing black heels, for example, choose a handbag that has some black in it to bring everything together.

TAILORED TROUSERS

A pair of unfussy black or grey wool trousers with slanted front pockets is timelessly chic. **Think Katharine Hepburn.** Wear them with a crisp blouse or cashmere sweater for effortless elegance.

Surefire ways to avoid that 'JUST-THROWN-MY-OUTFIT-TOGETHER' look...

There's no mistaking the look. Whether you've neglected your jewellery, foregone make-up or taken a risk on not ironing your top in your rush out of the door, **there's not much you can do to remedy the situation once you're on your way to work**. So unless you fancy stopping off at the early-opening dress shop on the way in and re-inventing your look in the company ladies room (not the best way to make smart purchases and it rarely, if ever, compensates for poor planning, no matter how much money you throw at the problem) you need to get organized. Here are a few tips to get you organized to avoid those early-morning panic stations.

★ No matter how tired you are, lay out your clothes the night before work – it'll make the mornings seem much less daunting.

★ Always make sure your favourite, any-occasion suit or dress is clean, ironed and hanging in the wardrobe. Then at least you'll always have one outfit to hand that you feel comfortable in and know looks good.

★ Don't experiment when you're in a rush. Five minutes before you leave the house is not the best time to try a new look.

★ Plan a five-day work-week wardrobe. This will trully alleviate the stress all week long, and if the weather changes, simply have some back-up options to swap short sleeves for long.

★ Take care of yourself before anyone else. Learning to get up a little early if necessary to shower and dress yourself first before any demands from children or a partner will mean that it's less likely for you to throw any-old-thing on at the last minute.

★ Look for knits and cottons that are blended with synthetic fibres such as polyester, rayon or spandex. They show wrinkles less and you can often get away without ironing them!

The TOP TEN FASHION CRIMES to avoid at all costs

1 Skirts that are so short they become indecent when you sit down.
2 Tops that reveal too much cleavage.
3 Crop tops that show your stomach if you're over 20.
4 Skirts or trousers where the hem is hanging down.
5 Anything that is a size too small.
6 Dirty shoes or sneakers.
7 Clothes that haven't been ironed.
8 Clothes with dirty marks/baby sick/ kid's paint on.
9 G-strings that show above your jeans when you bend over.
10 Bras that are so ill-fitting they create a 'four boob' effect.

School-Run Style

When your kids hit nursery or school age, what the other mothers wear on the journey to drop off their little darlings can be a real eye-opener. These days, not only are mothers expected to keep the house nice, their kids clean and tidy and their men happy, but **they are also expected to look young, trendy and sexy.** In fact, the school run can sometimes feel a bit like entering a beauty contest – clothes are often up-to-the minute, make-up immaculate and hair perfectly coiffed. Here's how to make sure you look great without appearing as if you're trying too hard.

KID-FRIENDLY CLOTHES

You do a lot of bending down, running and sitting on the floor in your clothes, so think hard before wearing anything that restricts movement or that can easily crumple or stain. **Being practical doesn't mean you can't be stylish:** in winter sharp tailored trousers have their plus points – you won't have to worry about ladders in tights (pantyhose), cold legs or trying to run in a pencil skirt. In warmer months, a floaty dress or skirt and top looks clean and fresh.

BAG THE RIGHT BAG

Tiny credit-card size handbags are oh-so-cute but utterly useless for the average mum. Many totes are available in handy large sizes that still look stylish. **One big bag keeps things more organized,** especially when you may be also be juggling a violin, sports bag, lunch box and homework.

MATCHY MATCHY

However cute you think you look, **never match your clothes to your children's.** Even wearing colours that are the same are as big a no-no as matching your clothes to your partner's. Your child may be small, but she or he is an individual with their own personality to express.

What TO WEAR...

1. **Keep it simple;** you don't want to look as if you've tried too hard. Think effortless chic!
2. **Choose brightly coloured,** well-fitting T-shirts or cotton shirts for a crisp, modern look.
3. **Pull on some jeans** – as long as they fit well, they will always look fashionable.
4. **A stylish coat** in the winter can hide a multitude of sins, so invest in a good-quality, well-tailored new coat each season. It will add instant class to an outfit. Best of all, no one will ever know if you're still wearing your pyjama top underneath!
5. **Wear clean white sneakers** or flat ballet pumps to complete the casual but cool look.

What NOT TO WEAR...

1. **A miniskirt.** Leave that to the 20-something mums!
2. **Very high heels.** You'll just look silly tottering along with your kids in the morning. Save your Manolos for parents' evenings.
3. **Too much make-up.** It might look good in your bedroom mirror, but in the cruel cold light at the school gates it will make you seem older and overdone.
4. **Anything sparkly or over-fussy.** Eveningwear always looks silly and excessive in the morning.
5. **Lots of bling or logos.** Remember those with class don't feel the need to show it off, so don't do the school run laden with gold and diamonds – no one will be impressed.

Kiddie FASHION STAKES

The start of the school year is fraught with activities, not least the hurdle of buying school clothes. Here are a few tips to **get you through the buying stage without tears, tantrums** and cries of 'I'm not wearing that!'

Know the school dress code. Even if your child does not have a school uniform, there will be other restrictions, such as jewellery and suitability of clothes, especially a sport kit. To be forewarned is to be forearmed, so make sure you know all the requirements.

Don't repeat buy. Look thoroughly through your child's wardrobe. If they already have something – or an older sibling has – that they can use, don't buy another.

Try online or mail-order shopping. Avoid the tiresome journeys to the shops and endless trying on whenever possible. There are internet shops and catalogues that fit standard sizes plus a few that sell roomier fits. Many of your favourite shops are online.

Let them be creative. Schoolwear can be restrictive, so permit your children some little luxuries for self-expression, whether hair accessories, scarves, badges, shoe styles or even just a haircut – as long as they adhere to school rules.

Watch the weather. Be prepared for all eventualities of rain, snow and wind. Having the appropriate outer wear is critical for keeping your child safe and healthy.

Demonstrate your own unique style. Like everything, you are a role model for your children and if you take pride in your appearance, so will they. Try to keep a handle on any neuroses though – you do not want to nurture a fashion victim.

Managing Maternity-wear

Some woman love being pregnant and can't wait to show off their bump. Many, however, spend the entire nine months feeling like a fat, flustered frump. But it doesn't have to be like that. **It is possible to look great when you're expecting,** and when you look good, you feel fabulous too. Here are some tricks to ensure a stylish and comfortable pregnancy.

CHOOSE
HIPSTER PANTS

Forget maternity pants. Choose ordinary, low-rise cotton pants that **sit comfortably on your hips and avoid the whole belly area.** You may find that you only need to go up one or two sizes from your normal size.

WEAR A
GOOD BRA

This is one item you will definitely need to invest in. Go to your nearest department store and get professionally fitted for free – **it will make you feel a million times more comfortable.** Be prepared to get re-fitted as your breasts grow over your pregnancy.

DRESS IN
LAYERS

You may feel like a walking hormone and because you are also circulating a lot more blood than usual **you will feel a lot hotter.** Dress with this in mind. If you must wear a heavy sweater, wear a light shirt underneath so that you can shed it during the day.

COMFORT
IS KEY

The last thing you need when you are pregnant is hassle. **Stick with soft, loose clothing** that allows the skin to breathe and is easy to wash and wear. To ensure this, check care instructions religiously before you buy.

DON'T BE AFRAID OF
MATERNITY CLOTHES

Don't frustrate yourself by trying to expand waistlines with safety pins and extra buttons. **Accept that buying maternity clothes will be inevitable.** Remember, the more wear you are able to get out of them, the better your investment will be. So, as soon as you can't zip up your favourite pair of jeans, treat yourself to the comfort of maternity jeans – no one else will be able to know the difference, but you will certainly feel it.

BUY THE RIGHT SIZE

When shopping, be sure to select your pre-pregnancy size. Maternity clothes are designed this way. After all, your arms and legs don't get longer and your basic body structure will remain the same. **Well-made maternity clothes will give you the extra room only where you need it** – belly, bust, hips and armholes – while maintaining the pre-pregnancy proportions of your ordinary size range.

GO FLAT
FOR COMFORT

Yes, your feet may get bigger when you're pregnant – amazingly, by as much as one-half sizes. The added weight of baby won't make those heels any more pleasant to wear either. Although heels are fine for special occasions – occasionally – **adopt a comfy, stylish pair of low-heeled shoes or flat shoes** for everyday wear. Your feet will thank you!

SHOP ONLINE

You can buy extensive online collections from a variety of maternity fashion websites. This way you **get what you like at the best prices** and save your aching back and feet from pounding the high street in the process.

KEEP YOUR OWN IDENTITY

Your style before your became pregnant should continue to be your style during your pregnancy – after all, you are still the same person. **Never wear something when you're pregnant that you wouldn't wear when you are not**.

TREAT YOURSELF

Accept the fact that your body is changing, and pamper it. If **you look good, you feel good,** so get a good haircut and enjoy a manicure or massage.

THREE WAYS to LOOK GREAT during pregnancy

1. **Keep it simple.** Stick to clean, simple lines and classic cuts. Don't wear large or busy patterns that overwhelm your new curvy frame.

2. **Show off your curves.** Dare to wear a slightly lower neckline than usual, or a blouse that clings. Be proud of it: gone are the days when women felt they had to hide their bumps.

3. **Go with the glow.** Moisturize daily and gently exfoliate your skin once or twice a week to keep your skin radiant and smooth.

Post-pregnancy Fashion Power

As a new mum the pressure to get back in shape, and fast, can be overwhelming. All those irritating celebrity mums who seem able to squeeze into skin-tight jeans within weeks of giving birth only intensify this feeling. But **don't feel you are a failure if your old clothes seem a little tight immediately after your baby is born.** This is perfectly normal and healthy. Do a little post-pregnancy shopping instead and buy a couple of comfortable transition outfits that will help take the pressure off and make you feel good until you're back in shape.

It can take time to lose those last few baby pounds, but in the meantime, there's no reason why you shouldn't look sexy. It's simply a question of enhancing your assets and disguising the wobbly bits. Here's how.

Choose simple, well-cut dresses with detail in the neck area. This will draw the eye up and away from your tummy area.

Wear suits with long jackets that come down to mid-thigh and boot-cut or wide-leg trousers.

Avoid short skirts – just below the knee or calf-length is much more flattering.

Stick to neutral colours, such as black, grey or navy, they will hide a multitude of sins. You can add splashes of colour with cardigans, scarves or pashminas.

Flirty Fashion – How to Look Sexy Without Dressing Like a Porn Star

So you're feeling sexy and flirty and you want to dress to impress, but you don't want to look like you're trying too hard, and **you definitely don't want an outfit that says 'I'm here for the taking'.**

Sexy without being tarty – it's a delicate balance to strike. **How do you work the sexier garments into your daily routine** without looking as if you're trying to be a glamour model?

The trick is to **combine sexy with casual, comfy and feminine.** Here's how to do it…

OUT with the GIRLS

A night out on the town with your girlfriends usually means dressing up to the nines, dancing and meeting a lot of men. These evenings call for a look that makes you feel sexy, without getting into a 'who can wear the skimpiest outfit' contest. **Choose classy, subtly sexy outfits – you'll look far more seductive** than if you bare too much flesh. A pretty, sparkly top with jeans and heels is ideal if you're planning to go to a bar, or choose a slinky, but not too short dress if clubbing is on the menu.

To WORK

Forget frumpy jeans or out-of-style suits. Looking good will help prove to the younger women in the office that you can still teach them a thing or two about looking sexy, stylish and confident. Also, it will help show your boss you are confident about every aspect of yourself.

A timelessly sexy but smart look is the shirt and skirt combo. **Choose a shirt that is fitted to the extreme.** That means that you keep going down a size until the buttons over your chest start to pucker. Then buy the shirt that is one size above that – guaranteeing the tightest shirt possible without looking like you've grown out of it. The idea being that a close-fit on the bust gives the shirt a casually sexy and inviting aura.

Forget miniskirts if you want to be taken seriously. A fitted, pencil cut will show off your curves far better.

In the same way you found your sexy shirt, use this sizing guide for finding the perfect trousers or skirt. Try on the smallest pair possible and then look at your bottom. If you can see the outline of your pants, or the seams are bursting, they are too small. **Go up one size at a time until you see a smooth, yet curvy silhouette.**

WORKING IT when you're working out

If you're hoping to meet the man of your dreams, the gym can be a good place to start. But **there's nothing worse than an over-sexy outfit while you exercise.** Men are more inclined to notice those of us who work it right while we are working out. That means showing off the curves, lifting the chest and sucking in the stomach.

A good sports bra top is perfect for showing off your hard-earned physique while offering the support you really need. Couple the top with a pair of shorts or jogging bottoms and you'll be queen of the gym. **The trick is to watch for unsightly underwear lines** – if the worst comes to the worst, leave your pants in the locker room!

On a HOT DATE

The most important thing about looking sexy on a date is that you don't look as if you've tried too hard. **You want to look like you wake up, eat and sleep looking just as sexy** – he doesn't need to know that you spent an hour at the hairdresser's and another two hours getting ready.

Baring too much flesh is a first-date no-no – while you might get your date interested that night, if you go out looking like an erotic dancer, he'll be interested for all the wrong reasons. Instead you need to look 'accidentally sexy'. Remember the following three tips.

1 *Invest in a great-fitting bra*
It's important that your bra fits perfectly and supports and shapes your breasts well – whatever their size. So take the time to go for a fitting at your local department store. As for choosing a sexy bra, the detail is in the fabric and trimming. Satiny fabrics look best under outer apparel because nothing will snag over them (as opposed to lacy bras, for example, which show through knits). If you think your bra might peek through, find one with a pretty trim.

2 *Show some leg*
You don't need a miniskirt to show off smooth, bare legs, just great shoes or boots. But if a mini is your thing, pair one with a looser-fitting, high-neck top and flat shoes. Remember that if you show off your legs you should keep your cleavage covered up and vice versa.

3 *Draw attention to your neck*
Wearing blouses and sweaters that emphasize your neck and collarbone can be just as sexy as exposing your cleavage. Pay homage to your upper chest by wearing a top with a neckline that doesn't dip beneath your breasts. This will draw his eyes to your neck. The idea being to hint at what is concealed.

HERE IS THE FINAL CHECKLIST FOR
LOOKING SEXY NOT SLUTTY...

1 **Wear soft, inviting, touchable fabrics** all the time. Silk or cashmere are particularly sensual.

2 **Steer clear of the obvious** – like ultra-short skirts or see-through tops. Let well-cut clothes do the talking.

3 **Always try on your clothes carefully** and don't be afraid to go down or up a size if it helps with the fit.

4 **Team something sexy** with something more conservative to give just a suggestion of sensuality.

5 **Choose smooth, streamlined underwear** – bulging bras or visible panty lines are NEVER sexy.

Shop 'Til You Drop

Making fashion mistakes is something all women do and desperate housewives are no exception! In fact studies by UK consumer group Mintel suggest women in the UK waste enough money a year on clothes, shoes and fashion accessories they never wear to pay for a week-long holiday abroad.

Part of the problem is that, even by the time we reach our 30s and 40s, **many of us haven't worked out exactly what our personal style is**, and divorce, having kids and changing jobs can all mean it's time for a change of image.

The key is to **learn how to choose clothes** that match your tastes, suit your lifestyle, flatter your shape and work within your budget.

Get READY...

Scan your wardrobe to see what is missing. Look at the items that you never wear, then at what you always wear and work out what you need, but don't have. **Create a list of key items you feel you must have now.** If you know that a classic item in your wardrobe still works for you, include it on your list. Replace the item if it looks worn, or, if possible, buy it in another colour.

The key to spring-cleaning your wardrobe is throwing things out, even if it is only to create space for sales bargains. But before you can get rid of things, you need to know exactly what you've got.

Take everything out and only put back what you really like. If things are too small, look long and hard at yourself and remember that if you need to go down a whole size to get into them, it will take you at least three or four months. Realistically, you won't wear those clothes again until next winter, by which time you will probably be so pleased with your new, slimmer self that you'll want to go out and buy a whole new set of clothes!

SPRING-CLEANING YOUR WARDROBE

1 **Only keep clothes that make you feel good.** Will you honestly diet into that size small dress? If not, stop torturing yourself and give it to charity.

2 **Invest in proper coat-hangers,** hanging bags for sweaters and shoe-trees.

3 **Organize your wardrobe** in whatever way makes sense to you. For example, everyday and special-occasion clothes, or by colour or garment type.

4 **Professionally dry-clean,** repair and pack away special-occasion clothes.

5 **Look at the previous years' sales mistakes** and don't make them again!

THINK OF A NUMBER
AND STICK TO IT

Before any shopping trip, **decide how much you can realistically spend** and then give yourself a 10–15 per cent leeway for must-have splurges.

YOU CAN'T
HURRY, LOVE

Don't go shopping when you haven't got time – an hour is not enough. **Avoid shops when you are preoccupied with other things** or you are having a bad hair day. Mistakes are just waiting to happen.

DRESS FOR
SUCCESS

Dress appropriately and make sure you **wear clothes that are easy to put on and take off.** If you are looking for a sexy evening dress, don't wear trainers. Keep your clothes simple but ensure that you wear things that make you feel confident.

...GO!

Once you've prepared yourself for a successful shopping day, here are a few tried and tested methods to make **sure you get what you want.**

STAY FOCUSED

Be careful not to get sidetracked by **falling in love with an item you don't need.** It's highly unlikely that these items will become wardrobe staples and will probably end up on a back shelf unworn.

BE HONEST
WITH YOURSELF

How does it fit? How does it look on you? How do you feel? Do you feel confident? **Do you love the piece because it is 'in',** because it gives you 'the look' or because it says something about who you are?

Don't buy a colour just because it is trendy or because it looks good on your best friend. Look at the colour against your skin, your hair and your eyes.

Avoiding SALE DISASTERS

Sale bargains that seem too good to miss but end up never being worn are **the biggest waste of your hard-earned cash imaginable.** Here is how to hunt down a real must have and avoid wasting time and money on items that will never see the light of day.

SIX STEPS TO SPEEDY SALE SHOPPING

1   **Decide what you are looking for** and stick to it.

2   **Only buy things in the right size** and that fit perfectly – the only exceptions being trousers or skirts that simply need taking up in length.

3   **Think comfort.** Anything that feels uncomfortable when you first try it on will be murder by the end of the day!

4   **Stick to classics.** That orange and blue miniskirt might be very this season, but how will it look next year? You are better off sticking to simple, timeless pieces.

5   **If you can't see yourself wearing it on at least three different occasions,** don't buy it (unless it is sportswear or a wedding dress of course!).

6   **Don't buy anything in a sale that you would not pay full price for.** It's not a bargain if it's not great and won't fit into your existing wardrobe.

Shopaholics Anon

Getting into debt is easier than ever these days with credit card companies happy to lend what seems like limitless amounts of money – regardless of whether customers can afford to pay it back. So if your shopping habit has spiralled out of control, here are five ways to **regain command of your finances – and swap debt for wealth...**

1 SIMPLIFY YOUR FINANCES

If you're overwhelmed by the number of statements you receive for credit cards, store cards, unsecured loans and bank accounts, close some of the accounts and consolidate others. The simpler your financial life, the easier it is to keep track of.

2 STOP WASTING CASH

Add up the money you have spent on clothes, accessories or cosmetics you only used a few times. Go shopping for groceries with a list and stick to it so you don't end up throwing away food each week. Remember that's actually hard-earned money you are throwing out.

3 DON'T PAY YOUR BANK

Consolidate as much of your high-interest debt onto a 0 per cent or low-percentage credit card and commit to paying it off by the time the introductory interest rate ends. But don't transfer repeatedly. Get out of debt and stay out.

4 RECYCLE YOUR MONEY

Have a look around your house, collect all the items you are not using and sell them at a car-boot or garage sale or on eBay. Use the money to whittle away at debts or put it into a savings account.

5 BUY THINGS THAT HOLD THEIR VALUE

When you spend money on your house, think about whether you are adding value. When you are buying clothes ask yourself, if you were to sell it later, how much you could recover. The eBay website has a pretty healthy trade in second-hand designer shoes and handbags, which could be a great way to recoup some of the money you've paid out.

Stay IN CONTROL of your credit card

Credit cards can be great so long as you don't let them own you. **There can be some real benefits to having cards**, but it all depends on how you use them. If you find yourself unable to pay your bill off each month and can only watch it steadily grow, you're not in charge of your spending.

BEST WAYS TO USE YOUR CARD

⭐ Charge your **big purchases as soon after the billing cycle closes** as possible. That way you have an entire month before your bill comes and you have to settle the balance.

⭐ Get rid of all but one of your credit cards, which you can use for big purchases. You should try to **pay off the balance each month,** thereby avoiding interest and an escalation of debt.

⭐ If you don't clear the balance on your card each month, **be careful about what you put on it.** Try not to put groceries on it, because you'll eat them right away but could end up paying for them for months as the interest slowly increases the price of your food.

HOW TO SPEND LESS ON CREDIT CARDS

⭐ If your card company charges an annual fee, ask that it be removed. Many companies don't charge a fee, so you can always switch to one of these, and some companies will remove the fee if you just ask.

⭐ Make the most of perks like free insurance or air miles with every purchase. As long as you're using your card responsibly, sign up for a mileage card or a card that offers money back with each purchase.

⭐ If you accidentally make a late payment, call and ask if the late fee and interest can be removed. Most companies will do this once if you ask.

⭐ If you constantly make late payments because the bill is due two days before you get paid, call your credit card company. Ask whether your billing date can be moved to a week later so you can deposit your wage and still pay the bill on time.

⭐ If you normally pay on time, try asking whether your interest rate can be lowered a percentage point or even a fraction of a point.

CHAPTER 3

Career and Family

The Juggling Act

It's the ultimate dilemma for twenty-first-century women: **how to successfully juggle career, family and love** without ending up so frazzled you can barely keep your eyes open long enough to kiss your kids goodnight, let alone have sex with your husband.

It's the **little things that can make a difference** when it comes to life running smoothly that can mean creating a better morning routine, staying involved in your child's life while you're at work, or making more of your evenings at home. Here are some ideas to help you get the busy mum balance right.

Make Mornings Less Manic

★ Follow the **same consistent routine** each day so your children know what to expect.

★ **Get up before your kids** to exercise or have a quiet cup of coffee and get showered and dressed.

★ Set out your kids' clothes the night before so there's **no arguing about what to wear.**

★ Let your children do as much as they can by themselves – get dressed, brush their hair or pour themselves cereal. This will **help them feel more independent** while freeing you up to do other things.

GET ORGANIZED ahead of time

★ **Prepare as much as you can before you go to bed:** check school bags, get out school and work clothes, make packed lunches, run and empty the dishwasher and make a list for the nanny if you have one.

★ Create a **designated drop-off/pick-up area** for shoes, coats, bags, sports equipment and anything else that's needed every morning.

★ Near the door, place a file or folder with all school notices and reminders, which you can review every evening. Put any plans you need to put into action on a **daily to-do list** for the next day and prioritize them.

★ Hang a clock in a place where everyone can see it and make sure every family member is aware of their latest **'out-the-door' time.**

★ **Organize shifts** for breakfast, bathtime and so on to keep everyone moving – this way no one will be wasting time waiting.

While You're Working

★ Go on **school field trips or volunteer in the classroom** if you can take time off from work.

★ Stay in touch with your child's teacher or nanny by phone and email. Ask your childminder to keep a diary of your child's activities and any homework, upcoming events or milestones so you **don't feel like you're missing out** on their growing up.

★ Don't delegate school or nursery dramas, musical concerts, parent-teacher meetings or sports days to your child's carer – make sure you or your partner **show up for all important events**.

Make Evenings Count

- Give yourself and your kids **time to relax and unwind**. Make kid-friendly meals in advance or cook something quick and easy so you don't spend the whole time stuck in the kitchen. And treat yourself to dinners out or takeouts from time to time.

- Make it a rule that you **turn off the TV** and talk about your day as a family during dinner.

- **Stick to an evening routine** so your kids know what to expect, but factor in fun and time to snuggle, too.

Keep your LOVE LIFE alive

Make sure you **spend time with your man**, even if it's just reading or watching TV. Phone calls and emails during the workday can also make you feel closer and like you're part of each other's lives.

Schedule **lunch or dinner dates together** at least once a week. And don't feel guilty about sometimes putting the kids to bed early so you have more time to yourselves.

Creating 'Me' Time

Work takes up so much of our lives these days and it seems **working mothers bear most of the burden**. We spend an average of two hours more than our partners each weekday, and three hours more on weekends, caring for the kids and doing the housework. No wonder it's difficult to find a healthy balance, which can make for some tough life choices.

Begin right now by **taking the time to reflect** on the quality of your family life and think about how you can start taking steps to improve obvious problems. Here's an eight-step plan to get you back on track.

1

BANISH STRESS

It's impossible, even undesirable, to eliminate all the stress from our lives. Stress, when properly managed, can actually motivate us and get our adrenaline pumping. But if it is not properly defused or a situation feels like it's spiralling out of control, **stress can begin to damage our health**.

Identify what stresses you out on a day-to-day basis – whether it's your boss or your husband's lack of help around the house. Then, see where you can remove or ease the stress triggers from your life. If they can't be eliminated altogether ask yourself, **is it possible to change your reaction** to them so they don't faze you as much?

2 MAKE IT EASY ON YOURSELF

We all tend to overfill our diaries and end up rushing from one place to the next or cancelling at the last minute. Remember, you don't need to be busy every minute of the day. **Don't make a commitment unless it is important** to you. Get in the habit of saying no to things you don't want, or don't have time, to do – and don't feel guilty about it. And don't be a slave to the phone – that's what answering machines are for.

3 HAVE FUN

All work and no play will make anyone a dull girl. Allow your free time to decrease and you'll notice your relationships begin to suffer. So take time out to have fun. Read with your child, cuddle your baby, play tag, watch a favourite movie with your man.

Be really there for that moment. **Show your family how important they are** to you by spending some one-on-one time with them every day.

BE DISCIPLINED

Be as **firm about your out-of-work time** as you are in the office. When you leave work for the day, try to put career concerns completely out of your mind for the rest of the evening. Fix a certain time in the morning when you will permit yourself to think about work again and instead devote your thinking space to home and social life.

SHARE THE LOAD

Let's get one thing clear, partners and children – even toddlers – can help out around the house. Sit down as a family and decide where the household cleaning priorities lie, and **assign jobs.** Do you really care if your blinds haven't been dusted in a month? Does anyone else notice?

Giving your children age-appropriate duties helps them to develop independence. And sharing the load will result in **more time for everyone** and a calmer, more peaceful home.

SLOW THE PACE

Sometimes we all feel that we're being pulled in too many directions and are about to break. If you feel there just isn't enough of you to go around, ask yourself, 'What is the most enjoyable and rewarding thing I could be doing for me and my family?'

Don't give another thought to wasting your precious time on activities that are meaningless to you. Instead, put the **focus on what is really important in your life.** Have realistic expectations of yourself and others. Learn to be adaptable and let go of what you no longer need.

PAMPER YOURSELF

Look after your body and it will easily cope with the stresses of everyday life. A well-balanced diet, regular exercise and plenty of sleep can work wonders at **boosting your energy levels.**

TAKE STOCK REGULARLY

Before you go to bed, take a few minutes to think about the day that has just passed, and to review the day ahead. This is also a great time to think about anything you want to achieve as it will help you stay focused. **Keep an eye on how things are going** and planning for the future will help you feel more in control of your life.

Stay at Home or Back to Work?

One of the most difficult decisions for new parents to make is deciding whether to return to work or stay at home with the baby.

For some, the choice is made for them, as **their finances dictate** that they have to go back to work. For others, many factors contribute to the final decision.

If you're able to stay at home, the rewards are many. One of the greatest benefits is being able to **watch your child grow up**.

But don't fall into the trap of believing that staying at home is necessarily better for your child than working. Especially if you know that, as much as you love your babies, you're going to feel **bored and frustrated** – which is not good for your child or you.

No matter what the outcome, women are often **plagued with guilt.** A surefire way to combat this is to make a choice, stick to it and, more importantly, accept it. And remember **not to judge other mothers** who make a different choice to yours.

Working from Home

Are you ready to take the plunge and be your own boss?

For most, cutting out the daily commute, endless meetings and office politics seems like a dream come true, but will the reality really suit you? **Are you ready to become your own boss** and work from home? Ask yourself the following seven questions to find out if this lifestyle would really work for you.

1 ARE YOU **SELF-RELIANT?**

People who make a success of working from home tend to be individualists at heart. They've either chosen to work independently, or, once becoming involuntarily self-employed, they discover that they like it.

2 ARE YOU **GOOD AT MANAGING** YOUR OWN **TIME?**

This is a vital skill to have when you are your own boss. There will be no one to chase you and make sure you meet deadlines – everything is down to you!

3 DO YOU **ENJOY VARIETY?**

Happy freelancers tend to tire easily of monotony. They prefer to choose their assignments, rather than performing the same tasks over and over again and working on your own means constant change and new challenges.

4 DO YOU WANT TO **LEARN NEW SKILLS?**

To work well at home it's often necessary to keep learning fresh skills in order to stay competitive and get enough new customers or clients.

5 DO YOU WANT A **BETTER BALANCE** BETWEEN YOUR **WORK AND THE REST OF YOUR LIFE?**

The majority of people who opt to work for themselves are in search of a better mix between their professional and personal lives. Since people who work for themselves control their hours, it's **easier to reserve time for family, hobbies and other personal interests.** Part of the beauty of being boss-free is working when you want or need to.

6 DO YOU **HATE OFFICE POLITICS?**

Getting out of a bitchy, competitive office atmosphere can hold appeal for a lot of people. **You can focus on your work** without the complex politics that preoccupy many full-time employees struggling to climb the corporate ladder.

7 CAN WORKING FROM **HOME** SUPPORT YOU **FINANCIALLY?**

Initially, most people who work for themselves will **find their income drops.** You need to sit down and work out what the minimum amount you need to earn every month is, and if you can make that.

If you want to be a part-time work-at-home mum, then divide your monthly income needs by 80 (20 hours a week for four weeks) and you'll see how much you'll need to be earning per hour – either being paid on a per-project basis or an hourly rate.

Take a look at your current outgoings and see what you can cut down on. Then **assess what you need to get started** – don't forget that, depending on the type of job you're planning on doing, you may already have the necessary items, such as a computer and a telephone.

How to make home-working
A SUCCESS

KEEP IN TOUCH WITH THE OUTSIDE WORLD

Without the social side of an office, at first you may find your days working at home a bit dull. You can minimize these problems by:

★ Making time to socialize and meet new people, particularly if you live alone. **It's easy to become a recluse** so don't fall into the trap. Go for lunches and early evening drinks.

★ If you're freelancing, **arrange the occasional meeting with those you work for** – personal contact is so much more memorable than email or phone conversations.

BE **KIND**
TO YOURSELF

Being surrounded by the other parts of your life makes it all too easy to be distracted. If you're in the habit of doing bits of housework whenever you're in during the day **educate yourself to ignore it.** When everyone in a household goes out to work it's easy to split routine jobs such as washing up and cooking on a whoever's-home-first basis. If you stay at home it becomes trickier.

Even in the most equal relationships one partner always has a **sharper eye for what needs to be done.** If that's you, you can easily end up with two jobs that seem to have no starting or finishing time.

★ Treat your working hours as seriously as you would time in an office.

★ Learn to ignore household jobs until you've finished your work.

★ Encourage kids and partners to help out more.

BE **PROPERLY EQUIPPED**

Getting set up well at home is an essential investment if you want to make a success of being your own boss.

★ **Don't settle for something that will do for now.** If you work at the kitchen table you'll waste a lot of time clearing away at night and then getting everything out again the next morning.

★ **Make your work area separate from your bedroom.** A space with a door that you can close when you want the rest of the world to leave you alone is best.

★ **Installing a separate telephone line** is an effective way of making clear distinctions between your work and home life. When you finish working let a machine answer business calls for you, likewise for personal calls while you're at work.

GET **HELP** WITH THE **KIDS**

If you're tempted by the idea of combining working from home with looking after a young family, think again. **You can't work productively with young kids at home** – they need too much attention. Don't feel guilty about using childcare if you're just working in another room in the house.

FIVE TRICKS to make home feel like A REAL OFFICE

1 **Use space that you can lock up** when you're finished for the day. If this isn't possible, at least make sure there's no chance that little hands can mess up your desktop.

2 **Get up half an hour earlier** and do housework before you start work.

3 **Cultivate a selfish streak** and learn to say no. Just because your house is the one nearest to school, it doesn't mean that you always have to be the one to pick up your friends' kids.

4 **Dress for work.** If you wear a baggy jumper and jeans every day, you'll end up feeling lazy and inefficient. Mark the difference between your work and free time by your clothes – you don't have to wear a suit, but sitting around in your PJs all day is not conducive to work!

5 **NEVER turn on the television.** Daytime TV is addictive and getting hooked is easy. For a little light relief, go for a walk or read the paper.

Climbing the Ladder and Hitting the Glass Ceiling

Despite all the progress women in the workforce have made in the last 50 years, **it can still be tougher for a woman to rise all the way to the top.** And once they get there, according to the latest figures, they're unlikely to be paid as much as their male counterparts doing EXACTLY the same job. So equality still has a long way to go.

Indeed, when it comes to working mums you would think that some companies were still living in the Dark Ages in terms of the lack of support on offer. But that doesn't mean you can't take control of your career. There is plenty you can do to boost your profile at work – and that doesn't mean having to stay late every night. Here are a few clever ways to **get yourself noticed...**

NETWORK SHAMELESSLY

You need to get known throughout the company, because that's a **good route to future promotions** and pay rises. If you're asked to head up a committee, pick people outside your group – and of course people you think it would be helpful for you to get to know.

But remember, work isn't the only place to network. Other parents at your children's school, neighbours, local merchants, and your kids' teachers and instructors all make a powerful and wide-ranging network that you can utilize. In fact, other mothers at the school and their husbands will bring you in touch with ever-widening circles of social, and potentially professional, contacts.

MAKE YOURSELF
IRREPLACEABLE

At your own workplace, try to predict what might be the next big area of development in your field. **Start teaching yourself the necessary skills** now, and be vocal about it. It's sure to heighten your profile at work.

DON'T TAKE
ON EVERYTHING

Choose the projects you take on carefully, and focus on doing them well rather than trying to be visible all over the place.

DO THE JOB
NO ONE ELSE WANTS

If there's a particular task no one else fancies, but it has the **potential to win you big brownie points,** should it succeed, go for it. Even if you're only half successful, you'll still be noticed as an enthusiastic person who is happy to take risks.

TAKE CONTROL
OF YOUR OWN CAREER

Promotion means **more than just coasting along** doing the minimum that's needed but secretly hoping someone will notice your untapped potential. Unless you're very lucky your boss is unlikely to devote much time to bringing you on, which means developing and getting ahead is up to you.

Getting Ahead as a Woman

How to BE ASSERTIVE
without being aggressive

Look at your friends and colleagues. **You can always tell who has power.**

A woman who uses her power wisely gives off the feeling of belonging in any work scenario. She's not afraid to look people in the eye and hold their gaze. She doesn't need to cultivate intimate work friendships and tends to remain friendly but a little aloof. She dresses smartly and never looks anything but well-groomed. She doesn't moan or complain and never brings personal problems into the office. Here are some ways to **boost your power quota at work...**

ACT AS IF YOU ALREADY HAVE WHAT YOU WANT

Calmly behaving as if you have what you're after means you start off in charge and are less likely to get flustered. **Stop being passive-aggressive** – people who feel they have no power often feel they have no time. If you sense you are constantly rushed, the problem may not be a lack of time but thinking you're not in control.

GET THE BALANCE RIGHT

There are times when you have to say no, and you're right to do so. But sometimes, **saying yes can be even more powerful.** Even if it means putting yourself on the line and pushing that bit further.

IF YOU DON'T ASK...

This is the simplest and most effective tactic. **Ask for more than you expect to get.** Most women end up asking for less and then are upset when they don't get offered more. Never ask for – or accept – less than you think you truly deserve.

How to get
WHAT YOU WANT

 ### 1 DON'T WAVER

Avoid coming across as wishy-washy about what you're asking for. All too often we apologize, make excuses, give long explanations or generally beat about the bush so that the person listening is given a very mixed message.

 ### 2 BE DIRECT

Work out in advance what it is that you want to say and then say it as clearly and directly as you can, with no extra frills. Sound as though you know what you want or what you think, and people will believe you and know where they stand with you.

 ### 3 SAY LESS

The fewer words you use, the bigger the impact. Powerful, effective women are always succinct. Remind yourself that clever people listen more often than they speak.

 ### 4 BE POSITIVE

Make sure that you are friendly and warm without being over the top. Smile when you ask someone to do something, and always thank them afterwards.

 ### 5 MAKE EYE CONTACT

Everyone will take you far more seriously, and be clearer about what you want if you look directly at them and give the conversation, however brief, your full attention.

Five tricks to KICK-START a flagging career

1 DON'T ASK QUESTIONS YOU CAN'T ANSWER

Yes, it's comforting to ask your boss when you lack confidence or feel you need their approval, but next time, ask yourself first. Will they be able to answer any better than you can? In most cases, probably not. You know your job better than anyone else; be resourceful and think things through first.

2 ONLY PRESENT A PROBLEM WITH A SOLUTION

It's annoying if people come to you with problems and expect a solution. So, equally, don't go to your boss with a problem if you haven't spent at least ten minutes thinking of possible solutions. It will impress your boss if you go to them with a tricky issue and then suggest ways to resolve it.

3 DON'T APOLOGIZE

Starting off with an apology makes you look weak. Instead, focus on what you've learned rather than what you've done wrong.

4 NEVER CRY OR SHOUT

Work is not the place to show your emotions. Don't ever send an email in a moment of anger or frustration. Write your response immediately, but don't send it. Wait at least half an hour, then re-read it. Nine times out of ten, you will have calmed down and can send a much more considered response.

5 GO THE EXTRA MILE

We all get asked to do things that aren't strictly in our job description. But taking on new challenges is a good thing. You may well learn something new and your boss will be impressed by your team spirit.

Moving ON UP

- Make sure you know your current job inside out.

- Find out everything you can about how far you can go in your company.

- Make the effort to get on with prospective colleagues in the department you hope to join.

- Smile – enthusiasm for the job is infectious and makes you good to be around.

- Always be punctual, smart and reliable.

- Don't be a clock watcher – bosses hate them!

- Take all training opportunities offered – and try to seek some out.

From Mummy to Manager – Survive the Switch

Going back to work after a few months off on maternity leave – or an even longer career break – **can be daunting.** Will you have lost touch? Have you forgotten how to do anything apart from play with toys and cook kids food?

Try the following tricks to ease the transition.

WORK OUT YOUR WORTH

Do a skills inventory and **list what you are good at.** Don't disqualify a skill or experience because you feel it isn't office related. So what if you were a stay-at-home mum, you may have organized parent-teacher meetings or a kid's birthday party. Both demonstrate your ability to be a leader and get things done.

GO BACK TO YOUR OLD JOB

This will make returning to work much easier. And if you enjoy what you do, going to work is less stressful. You know what to expect, the people won't be strangers – even the journey will be familiar. If you are not sure, **opt for part-time,** contract, or freelance work first and remember you can move on once you've got your confidence back.

LEARN ALL YOU CAN
WHILE AT HOME

Feeding the kids, changing nappies, and cleaning the house is a full-time job, but if you can spare the time, **read books or attend night classes** that can help you get up to speed in your chosen area.

RETRAIN
YOUR MAN

With your new job, you may find you have less time to devote to your husband and he may feel neglected. While he should get used to the fact, you too must **make sure you create space for him.** The male ego can be fragile, so be careful to include him in everything.

GET YOUR
KIDS READY

They are the ones who are likely to miss mum most. Be prepared for tantrums, but reassure them that you will be contactable. Always **let them know when you will be home** and make up for lost time when you get back. Remember, it's good for them to become more independent.

GET HELP

Don't try to be a superwoman and do everything. Be prepared for conflicts as everyone adjusts to the working schedule. Sit down with your family to discuss housework and childcare before you start work. **Make sure jobs are to be shared** with your partner or even farmed out to the older kids. And rope in grandparents or friends to help you if both of you have to work late.

What to Do if Your Boss is Younger than You

There is a good chance if you've taken a career break to have children that your peers will have moved up the career ladder while you were busy with your babies. **The key is not to be envious** – never think about having sacrificed your position for your kids. At least you've had a chance to bond with them and watch them grow up. If you produce results and prove your worth, you will be rewarded just as well as the next employee – and catching up with your peers should no longer be an issue. It may just take longer.

You may also find, on returning to work, that you suddenly have a boss who is younger than you. This can be a blow to your ego, but your life skills can complement their lack of work experience. You may find that due to the experiences you've been through **you have greater skills than a younger person** – better powers of negotiation, more extensive and powerful personal contacts, and a confidence born of learning to multi-task and cope under the pressure of many demands at once. If you are uncomfortable with your position, unsure of your status, or feel you've taken a giant step backwards, there are a few things you can do to make it easier.

Learn new skills so younger colleagues don't run circles around you. Coming back after an absence armed with a new cutting-edge skill that's only just being implemented will help you gain an edge and give you a confidence boost.

Change. Stop comparing the old ways to the new. **Keep your dress sense up to date.**

Coach your boss, no matter what their age. **Make yourself a resource.** Tell her what you know, but don't be condescending or patronizing.

Blow your own trumpet. This is the age of revolving bosses. Make sure as many superiors as possible know who you are and what you do.

Don't be afraid to discuss your concerns. Schedule a meeting with your younger boss to discuss the issues. Try to work it out. **Getting things out in the open will help** resolve things.

The key to success is **showing the younger manager respect from the start.** If your boss is a competent manager, then you work with her as you would with any other good manager. If she is not competent, it's likely she won't be in the position for long and you can then work with her successor – or get the job yourself!

Dealing With a Difficult Boss

We've all had bosses from hell.

Some are frightening, others just humiliate you – or maybe **no matter how hard you work, it's never enough.** The fact is you don't need a new job; you need a new boss. Here's how to cope with the five most common types.

THE **CARROT DANGLER**

They constantly hint at a pay rise or promotion if you work 'a little bit harder', then raise the bar and tell you to jump just a little higher every time you get close.

Solution

Ask your boss to put everything in writing.

THE
BULLYING BOSS

This boss is good at making you feel small, likes to shout and intimidate you.

Solution

To cope with this, nurture the boss by being friendly, but stand your ground when you need to – it's harder to bully someone you get on with and respect.

THE **CREEP**

They dislike most people in the office and always gossip about them.

Solution

Explain you don't like to hear negative things about others.

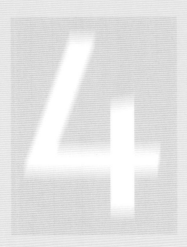

THE COMPLETE
WORKAHOLIC

They're devoted to their job and expect you to be the same – even if that means having no life outside work. And they're never understanding about child or family commitments or illnesses.

Solution

Set firm boundaries about what time you leave and don't be swayed. Get to know your rights as an employee and remind your boss if necessary.

THE 'MY WAY
OR THE HIGHWAY'

Another workaholic who has no insight or vision and cannot see the bigger picture. 'Right' means 'his/her way'.

Solution

Don't take it personally. This person treats everyone the same way. You will get your pay rise – not early, but you'll get it.

Make the Career Change You've Always Wanted

Being stuck in a rut means ticking over, **existing rather than living,** working just to earn money rather than for any real job satisfaction. To find out if this is you, answer these three questions.

1 Does your job excite and interest you?

2 Does it demand the best you are capable of giving?

3 Do you actively look forward to going to work most of the time?

If you answered no to any or all of these then **you're in a rut** and it's time to get yourself out of it.

Why? Because, comfortable as a rut is, hang around in it too long and you'll begin to believe that it's actually all you deserve and that life has nothing better to offer.

Everyone deserves a job that is challenging, interesting and rewarding, and the good news is, getting out of a rut is not as hard as you might think. Here's what to do.

1 BE HONEST ABOUT THE JOB YOU REALLY WANT

Deep down you probably have an idea, even if it's only sketchy, of what you want to do. What keeps us from admitting it is the belief that it's unattainable.

By telling yourself that you couldn't possibly run a company/write self-help books/teach Salsa dancing, then **you are making it impossible to fulfil your dream**.

2 SET GOALS FOR YOURSELF

Your ultimate goal is to make a living doing the thing you most want to do.

Now break it down into smaller steps, and then break those into steps, too.

For instance, if you work in an office but you actually want to be an acupuncturist you'll need to train. To do that, you'll need to find out what's involved, how much it costs and where to train.

3 GIVE YOURSELF TIME LIMITS

Set a time limit for achieving each of your goals. So, if you want to be a yoga teacher, give yourself two weeks to gather all the information together, three months to sign on a course and begin training and two years to qualify and set up on your own.

4 JUST DO IT!

The most important step of all. Get started and keep the momentum going. That means **doing something small every day** towards your goal. Make a call, write a letter, do some research, whatever is needed.

If there's something you dread doing or something that scares you, then do that first and don't give yourself time to dwell on it.

CHAPTER 4

Kids:
Living With
and
Without Them!

What to Do When Your Biological Clock is Ticking

'Should I have a baby?' 'And if so, when?'

These are two of the most important decisions that we face as women. But while they were pressing issues for our mothers in their 20s, the advent of better careers and later marriage means that today it's often not until we reach our 30s and 40s that these thoughts begin to loom large.

The other vital question, of course, particularly if you're over 35 or not in a relationship, is **'How can I have a baby?'**

While the odds vary from woman to woman, the **likelihood of conceiving and having a healthy baby declines after 35.** This is why the ticking of our biological clocks becomes louder than ever at this age. But many women today find themselves in their mid-thirties and still unsure whether motherhood is for them. Others know that it is, but don't have willing partners. Still more are trying to conceive and having trouble.

The resulting stress can be so intense that we're distracted from the other things that matter in life, such as our jobs, friends and relationships.

The key to minimizing the stress is to **make the choice that feels right for you and your partner** – regardless of what anyone else thinks. On the following pages you will find some advice on how to approach things.

Making the Decision...

THINK ABOUT IT, BUT
DON'T OBSESS!

Spending hours mulling over all the reasons to have, as well as the reasons not to, gets you nowhere. It will drive you crazy because the pros and cons often balance each other out.

Instead, think about parenthood at a deeper, more emotional level. Ask yourself, **'How much do I want to have the experience of being a parent?'** This is very different to just wanting to experience having a baby. You might love the idea of being pregnant but don't fancy the prospect of 20 years of feeding, clothing and supporting a child.

ASK YOUR MAN WHAT HE
REALLY WANTS

As a prospective father he needs to have **realistic expectations** and give you all the support you need. He has to accept that you'll no longer be able to take off for the weekend at a moment's notice, or decide to go out for dinner on a whim. And you'll have less money to spend on yourselves.

Most importantly, **make sure you're having a child for the right reasons.** A Band Aid baby will not heal an ailing relationship – parenting is stressful to begin with and may even expose fractures you never had reason to notice before, such as different discipline methods, parenting roles or family expectations.

What if he's NOT READY?

Give it time. If your partner is dead set against having children, don't force the issue or try to convince him – he needs to make that shift of his own accord. Whatever you do, **don't get pregnant 'accidentally'**. It may be tempting, but it is always a bad idea.

If you're holding out for a change of heart, **give yourself a deadline.** When that deadline arrives, though, be prepared for a heart-wrenching decision. You may have to decide what's more important to you – the baby or the relationship. The bottom line is: if you want kids, you need a partner who wants them, too.

If you do make a decision to leave, don't spend a year wondering whether you could have coaxed him into changing his mind, or if he would have changed his mind if you just happened to get pregnant anyway. Even if you did manage to coax him, kicking and screaming (or worse, silently resentful), into the baby thing you two could end up in a relationship undermined by unmet expectations and seething hostility for years to come.

Move on and go for what you want – you deserve it.

DON'T WORRY
IF YOU DON'T LOVE BABIES

Some women gaze on friends' children with intense baby lust, others find them hard to tolerate and have to force a smile when they see them. Neither attitude has any bearing on whether you'll make a good mother. **It's an old cliché but it really is different when they're your own.** That said, if you really don't feel any urge for children, and your partner agrees, you may find yourself at odds with the expectations of others. If your friends and family see you happy and enjoying a life, sans kids. They will be less concerned – the bottom line is your happiness. Be ready, though, for your feelings to alter, and for the possibility that your partner's feelings may change, too.

What if I'M SINGLE?

What's a lone girl to do when her biological clock is ticking and there's no man in sight? For some reason when single women start to talk about craving a child they get less sympathy. **There's a whiff of blame around the issue:** 'If you wanted a baby, why didn't you think about it five years ago? Why didn't you marry so-and-so? Maybe you have commitment problems.'

You may have spent years in a relationship or marriage that you believed would lead to a family, but it didn't. Or you may be a single mother but find yourself broody for another child. **So now what?**

There are options, such as adoption or using a sperm bank, and although most women are reluctant to become a solo parent, if you don't want to miss out on the experience of motherhood altogether it is an issue you need to give some serious thought to. Bear in mind that **most women who decide to have children alone say their only regret is not having made the decision sooner.**

Clearly, it's getting more and more acceptable for single women to have a child. Statistics show that the majority of single mothers are no longer teenagers – they are women of 30 and older.

Living with YOUR DECISION

Just because you've decided to try for a baby, it doesn't mean it's going to be plain sailing. Trying to conceive can be **one of the most stressful and heartbreaking experiences of a woman's life.**

If you have left it late it can be tempting to blame yourself – or indeed your partner – for not starting earlier. It's important to remember that you had good reasons for making the decisions you made in the circumstances you were in at the time. For example, maybe you and your partner decided to wait because you weren't able to support a baby. Don't lose sight of that and **try to stay positive.**

It's vital to **keep up other interests** so having a baby doesn't become your sole focus and purpose in life.

Coping with a New Baby

Making the change from being a couple to becoming parents is never easy, especially if you're doing it later in life. After a lifetime of looking after yourself and doing whatever you please, when you please, **it is suddenly hard to find time for yourselves.** Your sex life can change, you have to juggle the commitments of work and family, and you and your partner have to find a way of agreeing on how to bring up the kids.

It's an exciting but stressful time of adjustment, so it's important to remember to take good care of yourself. Here's some advice to help you cope.

SLEEP WHENEVER YOU CAN

This is without a doubt the most sleep-deprived you will ever be in your life, so it's vital you get as much shut-eye as is humanly possible. Whenever you can, **sleep while your baby sleeps,** and take turns with middle-of-the-night feeds and being in charge of the baby during the day so that you each have opportunities for uninterrupted breaks. Also try asking family or friends to come over and watch the baby while one or both of you new parents get some rest.

EAT SMART

Yes, feeding your baby is the most important thing, but **make sure that you eat healthy, regular meals yourself.** Get your family and friends to bring you lunch or dinner, or get them to help out with food shopping during this busy time.

GET OUT

Take a walk, sit in the garden, visit a friend – **whatever it takes to get you out of the house** – even if it is just for ten minutes a day.

BE REALISTIC

Don't expect too much of yourself. It doesn't matter if everyday chores like housework and shopping go out of the window during the first weeks. **Eventually, you'll get back into a regular routine,** so don't be afraid to ask for extra help in the meantime.

PAMPER YOURSELF

Make some time for yourself to keep you sane. This might mean asking your partner or a friend to look after the baby while you take a relaxing bath or shower, or perhaps arranging to be on your own for a few hours so that you can get your hair done, do some yoga or visit the cinema. Don't feel guilty, this 'me' time will help to make you a **more satisfied and patient mother.**

SPEND TIME WITH OTHER MUMS

It's very easy to feel isolated from the rest of the world when you're a new parent. Meeting up with others in the same situation can really help. **Join a local parenting group** or get together with some of the other couples from your antenatal class to share concerns and tips.

MAKE A FUSS
OF YOUR OTHER KIDS

Bringing in a new baby can create a lot of jealousy if you already have other children. To help combat this, make sure you **pay them attention every day,** in ways big and small. Let them know you love them. Try to include them as much as possible in getting to know the new baby.

ENJOY IT!

Above all else, ensure you **make the most of this very special time** – you won't be able to repeat it. Being a new parent is the most difficult and demanding role you'll ever have, but it will also bring you the most joy.

Don't Forget Your Man...

When a new baby comes along the love you feel can be so strong that **your partner gets pushed into the background.** Here's how to make sure he doesn't feel neglected.

Make time to talk. Agree on a time, it needn't be long, but choose a moment that suits you both, when you're not hungry or especially tired.

Take turns to listen to each other, uninterrupted, for a certain amount of time. One of you might talk for five or ten minutes about any particular problems and anxieties, while the other listens carefully without interrupting. Then the other partner is given an equal amount of time to do the same.

It is very important not to use language that blames or criticizes the other. The object is not to attack or undermine each other, but to **try and understand what the problems are.** Say, 'I feel abandoned when you go out after work instead of coming home to me and the baby', rather than, 'I'm furious that you spend so much time with your friends. You've never bothered to come home on time, and since we've had the baby things have got even worse!'

When you've listened to each other, go away and think about what has been said. Your first reactions may be anger and resentment; you might feel like crying. Let these feelings pass and focus on what your partner actually said so that you end up with a clearer understanding of his or her feelings. Then, when you're ready, use your insights to talk the problem through again calmly. **Try to move towards a solution that satisfies you both.**

If your sex life has suffered since the arrival of your little one, talk about it. Don't feel you can only discuss sex when you're actually in bed. It may be easier to chat about it when you're sitting on the sofa.

Book a night away together and spend some quality time remembering all the reasons you fancied each other in the first place.

Being an Older Mother

They say that life begins at 40 and for lots of women these days, so does motherhood. More women than ever are prepared to take the plunge post-35.

However, **some prejudices still exist about older mums** – often because of the increased risk of health problems for both mother and baby. But it's important to remember that, on the whole, babies are more likely to be planned and longed for by women in their 30s and 40s.

Older mums will often have **financial security** and, in many cases, a longer and more stable relationship, and the ability to take time out of a career with the possibility of returning to it later on.

Studies have shown that children of older mothers tend to do **better on ability tests** while other research shows that older women are also more likely to breastfeed.

But there are other considerations to bear in mind if you're having children later. For example, when your child is 10, you will be in your late 40s or early 50s, which could mean you have **less energy to cope with the demands of parenting.** You might also end up paying college or university fees when your peers are sitting back and enjoying their retirement. Problems cited among older women include infertility, higher rates of miscarriage, ectopic pregnancies, foetal and chromosomal abnormalities and the increased likelihood of a premature birth, stillbirth or neonatal death.

There is also a **greater risk of pregnancy diseases, such as pre-eclampsia,** and higher rates of miscarriage, foetal and chromosomal abnormalities, including Down's Syndrome. Children of older fathers also have higher rates of schizophrenia and genetic disorders. Although doctors recommend having a baby between the ages of 20 and 35, women are the ones making the decision and the rate of women having babies over 40, in the UK alone, has doubled in the last ten years. If you are considering a child at an older age, keep in mind that **you may need expensive IVF treatment.** Become well acquainted with all the risks so that you can make a well-informed judgement.

Travelling with Kids in Tow

A crying baby or a toddler throwing a tantrum when you happen to be in the middle of a flight or a long car journey is not much fun. But with a bit of **advance planning,** you can ensure everything goes smoothly and your kids are comfortable and happy.

Here is how to travel with your little one and make nightmares about screaming fits, wet nappies and general kid carnage a thing of the past.

TIME IT RIGHT

If your toddler falls asleep easily, **try to start your car, train or plane journey when they are at their most tired.** That way you can guarantee you'll get at least one hour's peace before you need to start entertaining them. If you're travelling with a new baby, start your trip when they have just been fed and changed.

BY CAR WITH A BABY

Whether you are popping to the shops or going on a long journey, your baby will need a safe car seat. Travelling with a baby on your lap in either the front or back seats is dangerous and in some countries even illegal. Remember, **never fit a rear-facing car seat in a passenger seat** that has an airbag as it could cause serious injury in an accident. Most new cars have a facility to lock off the airbag with a key, if need be.

BY PLANE

You may be able to reserve a sky cot for your baby on long-haul flights, so it is always worth checking with your chosen airline. Unless you pay for a separate seat, you will not have one, so the baby will be on your lap or in the bulkhead area for the duration of the flight. Many women travelling on their own with small children struggle. Learn to **utilize all the help on offer at the airport,** from porters who will assist with the luggage, pre-flight lounge areas for children and pre-boarding to using the onflight air staff who will help entertain the children, warm bottles and provide baby food. Smiles with your requests can go a long way toward helping you get a jump in the queue, but also look for fast-track immigration and customs. Ask if the flight is full at check-in – staff may be able to block out the seat next to you if there are spaces available.

KEEP **TODDLERS**
BUSY WITH BOOKS AND TOYS

All kids love music and it's a great way to keep them occupied on long journeys (especially in a car), so take a good selection of CDs you know they will enjoy. Another good trick is a **story-telling tape or CD** that they can listen to with headphones on. Also, try to buy new toys and books for the journey to surprise them.

Plan ahead for when your toddler is likely to need a break and work out your motorway exits. If it's a long trip, you're going to need a couple, which can add an hour or two on to your journey. Just accept it: **your journey time will be longer** but at least you'll also have the chance for a cup of tea and a break, and the kids can run around for a bit to use up some energy.

If you're travelling for several hours by plane, treat your toddler as if he is in a car. **Take plenty of books and toys,** and let him walk around the plane. Don't worry about the air stewardesses: they are used to dealing with kids and may even help out by talking to them, or showing them around the plane.

The ultimate MOTHER's TRAVEL KIT

Whenever and wherever you are travelling with your baby or tot, you will need to take supplies so you can feed, change and keep them amused. Here is what to include.

- ★ **Spare nappies (diapers)** – always take twice as many as you think you may need.
- ★ **Baby wipes** – great for faces and hands as well as bottoms.
- ★ **Changing mat** – or something clean and foldable such as a small towel to use as a changing mat.
- ★ **Extra clothes** – accidents happen, whether it's a leaky nappy (diaper) or spilt juice, so it pays to be prepared.
- ★ **Food and drink** – the only thing worse than a tired child is a tired and hungry one. So don't leave home without plenty of snacks for bribery, bottles of milk for baby and cartons of juice for thirsty children.
- ★ **Toys** – pack small toys that don't take up too much space and are easily replaced if lost or broken.
- ★ **Sunhats and sun cream** – delicate skin burns easily, so even if the weather doesn't look promising, make sure you have them ready to prevent sunstroke and sore, burnt skin.
- ★ **Swimming nappies (diapers) or bathing costumes** – if there's a good chance your trip will involve the opportunity to swim, pack them. You don't want to waste valuable time rushing around to find a shop that sells them.
- ★ **First aid kit** – make sure it includes waterproof Band Aids, antiseptic cream, paracetamol or ibuprofen, aftersun or calamine lotion to soothe any sunburn, insect repellant and some bite cream to stop itching if kids, or you, get bitten.

Keeping Your Cool

Taming toddler
TANTRUMS

So you've shouted, bribed and threatened, but still your kids won't stop throwing tantrums in the middle of the department store. And frankly, **you're at the end of your tether.**

Don't panic: there are some very effective tactics to ensure that you and your children don't end up becoming sworn enemies.

Toddlers aren't being bad when they have a tantrum; they are just acting their age. **Tantrums are a normal part of growing up.** However, if the tantrums start to become more frequent, you need to take action.

Here are some suggestions to help tame your tearaways.

STAY CALM
Nothing accelerates the intensity of a tantrum more than an angry parent. Seeing you lose your cool will only make it more difficult for your toddler to compose himself. So, **don't argue, don't shout and never lose your temper.**

SHOW THEM LOVE

Successful discipline can only happen within a loving environment. **Your toddler needs to feel important to you** and to know that he is loved, wanted, respected and cared for. If children don't have this, it's both difficult and unwise to try to change their behaviour.

BE CONSISTENT

Young children need to know what the limits are and exactly what is expected of them. They should sense that **both parents are in agreement** and, above all, in charge! To avoid confusing your child, discipline must be consistent and not dependent on you or your partner's moods.

DON'T GIVE IN

It might seem hard to believe but studies have shown that **your toddler wants you to be in charge** – so don't be afraid to be firm. No matter how tempted you may be, do not give in to his demands just to get some peace. Doing so will give your child confusing messages and feed and encourage the next tantrum. When you mean business, speak with conviction and, most importantly, see it through.

Many parents can't bear to see their children upset but **showing you mean business** involves knowing when to say 'no' and sticking to it. Giving in to tears allows a child to think: 'If I cry I can get what I want'.

TALK QUIETLY

Screaming over your toddler's yells will **only encourage your toddler to scream louder.** A gentle tone of voice assures your toddler that you are in control.

DON'T INTIMIDATE

It can be very intimidating to a child to have a bigger person towering over them. Bending down or sitting on the floor will help to even out the situation, making it **easier to communicate** with your child.

TRY DISTRACTION

Some children can be easily distracted during a tantrum while others only get more upset. If your child can be diverted, **try reading a book** or turn on a favourite tape, CD or video.

LEARN TO IGNORE

A powerful technique that tells your child their bad behaviour will not be tolerated is to ignore them. Develop selective blindness and deafness. Your toddler will quickly realize that it's no fun getting worked up when no one is watching.

The purpose is to give the undesirable **behaviour no attention at all,** and therefore make it happen less.

TAKE TIME OUT

For some children, especially older ones, 'time out' provides a much needed cooling-off period. Sending a child to his or her room for ten minutes not only shows them who is in charge, it also gives them **time to calm down** and take control of themselves and the situation.

REWARD GOOD BEHAVIOUR

Praise your child whenever you come home from a tantrum-free trip. **Reward good behaviour with love, fun and attention, not bribes.**

Banish 'Bad Mum' Guilt

For working mums, trying to find the elusive work–life balance is difficult. **There is no point in feeling miserable and stressed in both roles,** but not wanting to give up on either of them.

This means discovering a way of continuing to work without feeling like a nervous, guilt-consumed wreck who thinks she's failing, both as a mum and as an employee.

You may have to make some radical changes to your job. Investigate the possibility of doing **different hours that fit in better** with your childcare or the kids' school hours. If this isn't possible, consider changing employers. Do some research and find out if there are any companies in your field that offer mums more flexibility.

Maybe a **complete change of career direction** would help. For example, working in a financial company may not be as manageable as moving into a different sector such as PR or teaching. Don't be afraid to try something new. One solution is to become self-employed, either working part-time or from home.

Explore all the options thoroughly so you can find the right job that fits in with you and your family.

How to HANDLE IT

- **Accept that you are a working mum** and that isn't a bad thing.
- **Stop feeling guilty.** Banish all the inner voices that are saying things like, 'Good mums stay at home and always put their children first'.
- **Don't allow your colleagues to make you feel guilty.** You have to leave at 5 pm because you are a mother, not because you're shirking your work responsibilities.
- **Ignore the stories in the press** that say working mothers are damaging their kids. The most important factor in a child's development is not whether or not their mum goes to work but whether or not she is happy.
- **Get good-quality childcare.** You don't want to spend time at work worrying about your child. Look at a range of different nurseries and child minders before making up your mind.
- **Have the support of your partner,** so you know he is there to help lighten your load.
- **Don't aim for perfection.** It's not possible to be a working mum and have a spotless home. If you try and aim for this you'll burn yourself out. Get a cleaner, if you can afford it, and don't feel guilty about having takeouts some nights – as long as your kids are eating well the rest of the time the odd ready-made or fast-food meal will not do them any harm.
- **Explain to your kids,** when they are old enough the reasons why you go to work – it's so they can have all the nice things in life and the family can afford treats together.
- **Develop a good support network** of family, friends and neighbours who can help out in a childcare crisis. Offer to do the same for them.
- **Focus on the positive.** When you've had a bad day, make a list of all the positive reasons why you go to work and feel proud of the fact that your kids are happy and healthy.

Space for Everyone

Making MORE ROOM

A new addition to the family can result in you having to move to a larger home or add an extension to your existing one **as things get too cramped for comfort.** Unless we are lucky enough to live in a large house with enough rooms for a nursery and playroom, when we have kids our space can end up becoming dominated by their toys and games.

Most new parents are so engrossed in looking after baby and trying to get some sleep that the last thing on their mind is reorganizing the home. But, as your baby grows into a toddler, space becomes more of an issue as their belongings multiply ten-fold.

The only solution is to **get organized and set some rules** – in the long run it will reduce stress, and give you back control over your environment.

Seven ways to CREATE MORE SPACE

1 USE EVERY CORNER

Examine the spaces in your home to see what areas could be utilized more efficiently. A good place to start would be an alcove or the area above a bed. These spaces can be used far more imaginatively than as a bookshelf, and may be transformed into cupboards or other storage units.

2 ESTABLISH ORDER
– AND KEEP IT

It may sound obvious but when you're rushing around, tidying up is often the very last thing on your mind. However, **the effects of clutter on the mind can be quite dramatic,** bringing anything from mild stress to utter despair – particularly on Monday mornings when your kids' sports kits have gone missing... again!

Imagine how much easier life could be if you knew that every dark corner was in order, how much freer your mind would be without a backlog of 'things' waiting to be sorted out.

3 SET TOY RULES

Don't allow your kids to bring all their toys into your living area at one time. **Have a selection, divided up among boxes, and rotate them on a weekly basis.** This way the child has different toys to play with and your living space is still your own.

4 GET THE
KIDS TO HELP

Make tidying up part of your kids' routine. Paste photographs of their toys on the front of storage boxes so they can find them easily. And **make sure books are easily accessible.**

5 THROW IT
OUT!

Every time you buy something new for your kids – whether it's a toy or an item of clothing – **give something old to charity.** Clear out the clutter before you even consider looking at new storage solutions.

6 DON'T BE
SENTIMENTAL

Be discriminating. Set aside one small box for extra-special memories, such as kid's first pictures, photos, and so on, but **don't feel compelled to hoard everything.**

7 HAVE MUM AND
DAD SPACE

To help keep you sane, it's important that you have an 'Adults Only' area where you can get a bit of peace and quiet. This may be your own bedroom, a spare room or study – anywhere you can go to read, listen to music, or do other 'grown-up' things. **Don't feel guilty about excluding your kids** – it's important for them to understand boundaries early on. Plus, having a place to escape to will help reduce your stress levels and make you a far happier, more patient parent in the long run!

Childcare Dilemmas

CHOOSING the right CHILDCARE

Finding someone to care for your kids – be it a single child minder or a daycare centre – is **one of the hardest decisions a parent has to make.** Aside from the difficulty of being separated from your little one when you go back to work, you also need to feel confident that they will be well-cared for and safe.

CHOOSING A DAYCARE CENTRE, NURSERY OR PLAYGROUP

Make sure you **look around at least three or four places** before you decide where to take your child. Anywhere worth its salt will allow you to spend a morning sitting in and watching the kids with the staff, so you get a feel for whether or not it's somewhere you would be happy to leave your child.

Don't be afraid to ask them. Good childcare workers will expect questions and will also be prepared to show you the rooms and outside space that your child will use. Here are the nine most important things to find out...

1 Are the other children relaxed and do they seem to be enjoying themselves?
2 Are the staff listening to the children and joining in with their activities?
3 Do the staff seem friendly and genuinely interested in the children?
4 Does the centre look bright, clean and welcoming?
5 Is there a fun and safe outside play area?
6 Are there lots of interesting toys and activities for children?
7 Is the area child-friendly – with child-sized furniture and pictures the children have painted themselves on the wall?
8 Are the staff welcoming to you and the children in their care?
9 Are the facilities safe and secure, are the staff aware of who enters and leaves the premises.

CHOOSING A NANNY OR CHILDCARE PROVIDER

If you are looking for one-to-one care for your child it's even more important to **pick someone you trust and feel your child could bond with.** Here are some of the questions you should ask.

1 How long have you been working with children?
2 What training do you have?
3 Why do you enjoy your job?
4 How will you spend the day with my child?
5 Can I see your registration certificate?

COPING with SOMEONE ELSE
looking after your child

KEEP IN TOUCH

Call up regularly and ask how your child is doing and what they have been up to. Ask them to let you know of all their new developments and achievements so you don't miss any milestones.

KNOW WHAT YOU'RE DOING...

Tell them what goes on in your day. Your children will feel more connected to you if they know what you do all day. **Plan a lunchtime visit with your child to your office** so they can see where you work.

HAVE FUN WEEKENDS

Plan one-on-one activities and family outings. Going to the cinema and playing sports will **help make up for the time you're apart** and strengthen the bond with your kids.

MAKE TIME TO TALK

Chatting with your child at dinnertime and tucking them into bed every night will **help you to feel closer.** Just 20 minutes a day will make sure you are an important part of each other's busy daily lives.

TAKE TIME OFF WORK

Arrange to take holiday in order to attend any important function or activity in which your child is involved. **They will feel reassured** that they come first.

Help! My Husband Fancies the Nanny!

It's such a cliché. A man who's got everything, who's deeply in love with his gorgeous, successful wife, but just can't keep his hands off the nanny.

Why do they do it? Why jeopardize their marriage, home and family just for a bit of fun? And let's face it, nine times out of ten that is all it is – **no-strings sex in the comfort of their own home.**

Most men have no intention of bailing out to set up home with the nanny. But for some a young, pretty and available woman living in their house is **too much temptation to resist.** The irony is the nanny should be there to make your children's lives more stable, not break up your relationship.

But old-fashioned ideas about women being at home can be partly to blame. Some men with busy working wives see the nanny as being more willing to look after them than their wives, just like their mothers did. There's also the question of power. A man may feel more powerful with the nanny than he does with his high-earning, more assertive wife.

Another crucial issue may be the blurring of roles when another woman is allowed so intimately into the heart of the family. For some men, seeing someone else looking after their children can result in **confused boundaries about sexual desire and motherhood** – with catastrophic results.

How to prevent the
NANNY TRAP

Think long and hard before you hire a nanny. Bringing anyone new into your home will change the balance of it. Are you prepared for this? If not, daycare is an option to look at before inviting someone to live with you.

Don't choose a young, pretty nanny. Harsh, but true. Even if you have the most trustworthy husband in the world, do you really want someone who looks that good in your home every day? Think of the pressure to compete! If you need more justification, remember that older nannies will have more experience with kids.

Get a 'Manny'. One solution to preventing your husband from running off with the hired help is to employ a male nanny, or a 'manny' as some people call them. Just make sure you're not going to be tempted to start an affair yourself!

Parenting Masterclass

Being a parent is **one of the best and most rewarding jobs in the world,** but anyone who has done it would not deny that it's also one of the toughest.

It's a 24-hours-a-day, seven-days-a-week job that will be yours for the rest of your life.

Most people want to be **'the perfect parent'** – encouraging, loving, creative, dependable and fun. However, make sure your desire to be the perfect parent does not overshadow the simple joy of having kids.

What we all tend to forget is that no parent is perfect; we all make mistakes. **Even loving parents sometimes do things they don't mean to do,** such as slapping their child or shouting and swearing in front of them. It is part of being a parent.

So give yourself **permission to make mistakes.** You will not be able to forgive your children if you are unable to forgive yourself.

I get so frustrated sometimes. IS THIS NORMAL?

Of course – **all parents get stressed out.** Children take a lot of your time and energy. On top of that, you have the normal day-to-day problems that life entails, such as worries about your job, the bills or your relationships.

To be a good parent you have to **take care of yourself.** That means taking time out. Everyone needs a break from being a parent once in a while.

You and your partner should **take turns getting away.** For example, ask him to stay with the children so you can visit friends. Take turns sleeping late on the weekends.

It's easy to lose your temper with your children and **it's OK to feel angry,** but it's not fair to take it out on them. When you're really angry, have a break. Take the children for a walk or call a friend to come and give you a hand.

To smack or
NOT TO SMACK?

Smacking isn't the best way to discipline children. The goal of discipline is to teach children self-control. **Smacking just teaches them to stop doing something out of fear.**

There are many more effective techniques that do not cause physical pain and do not leave the parents feeling guilty that they might have hurt their child.

One good method for disciplining infants and toddlers is called **'redirecting'.** When you redirect a child, you replace an unwanted or bad behaviour with a good behaviour. For example, if throwing a ball inside the house isn't allowed, take your child outside.

With older kids, try to get them to **see the consequences of their actions** and take responsibility for them. For example, you can explain to your son that everyone had to wait for dinner because he didn't set the table when he was supposed to. Therefore, because he didn't set the table before dinner, he will have to wash the dishes afterwards.

The Good Mum Checklist

Show your love. Say 'I love you' to your children every day. Give lots of hugs and kisses.

Listen when your children talk. Listening to your children tells them that to you they're important and you're interested in what they have to say.

Make your children feel safe. Comfort and reassure them whenever they're scared. Show them you've taken steps to protect them.

Provide order in their lives. Keep a regular schedule of meals, naps and bedtimes. If you have to alter the routine, tell them about the changes ahead of time.

Praise your children. When your children learn something new or behave well, tell them you're proud of them.

Criticize the behaviour, not the child. When your child makes a mistake, don't say, 'You were bad'. Instead, explain what the child did wrong. For example, say: 'Running into the street without looking isn't safe.' Then tell the child what to do instead: 'First, look both ways for cars.'

Be consistent, making sure that the rules are the same all the time. Your rules don't have to be the same ones that other parents have, but they do need to be clear and consistent. If two parents are raising a child, both must use the same set of rules. Also, make sure that babysitters and relatives also know, and follow, your family rules.

Spend time with your children. Do things together like reading, walking, playing and cleaning the house. What children want most is your attention. Bad behaviour is usually their way of getting it!

Advice for Single Mums

As a single parent you may have come up against certain prejudices, but never let anyone make you feel any less valued than a two-parent family – there are actually benefits to being a **single parent.**

Having two parents under one roof is no assurance that harmony and love will prevail in the home – any more than having a mother at home during the day ensures well-adjusted, happy children.

It is the quality of the parent-child relationship that matters. Mothers who are fulfilled themselves are not only good role models for their children, but happier people, too. Research bears out what common sense tells us – happier women make happier mothers, whether married or single, working or at home.

In the past decade, several studies researched the effects of a mother's employment on her children. They found it was the **quality of childcare** and the closeness of the parent-child bond that was most important – not whether or not the mother was employed.

Yes, it is **difficult and challenging to raise children alone,** particularly if you're trying to pursue a career at the same time, but good, solid parenting has less to do with the number of parents in the home and everything to do with the quality of the parenting.

FEEL GOOD ABOUT IT

Start with a **positive attitude** and focus on the benefits of single parenting, such as less conflict and tension in the home. Many single mums who have just come out of a bad relationship treasure their newfound freedom and independence, and feel very excited about the future.

DON'T TAKE ON EVERYTHING

The single parent frequently feels overwhelmed by the responsibility, tasks and emotional overload involved in bringing up a child alone. **It is vital to ask for help when necessary.** Give your children appropriate jobs around the house and ask other parents for help with the school run or travel to after-school clubs.

BE A PARENT NOT A PEER!

Establish firm, clear boundaries that leave no doubt that you are the boss in the home. Single parents often make the mistake of allowing children to become equal partners or peers. This can cause real problems. Children need limits and consistent discipline that provides **clear expectations and guidelines** for behaviour. Allow children to be children, and find other adults for companionship and support.

RECOGNIZE YOU ARE DOING THE BEST YOU CAN

No matter how competent and loving you are, you are still only one person and you are **doing a job most agree is meant for two.** Do not allow your children to manipulate you by making you feel guilty. Remind them that you have to work together. Give yourself credit for a job well done.

CREATE STABILITY

Kids crave stability and security, especially if their world has just been turned upside down after a divorce. **Let them know how much you love them** and how proud of them you are. Be there for them when they need you or if anything goes wrong.

TAKE CARE OF YOURSELF

It's vital for your children's wellbeing that you take care of yourself, a stressed-out parent results in stressed-out kids. Of course there will be times when you feel like you need a break. Plan for this and **ask friends and family to help out** by babysitting for an afternoon so you can go for lunch or have a facial. You should also pay special attention to eating healthily, getting regular exercise and plenty of sleep – all of which will boost your energy levels and leave you more able to cope.

GET SUPPORT

Probably one of the most important things for any single mum to do is develop a wide network of people who can provide you with emotional support, companionship, help in emergencies, childcare or reality checks. Be selective and **choose reliable and caring friends** who will be there for you in times of need.

If you live a long way from your family, try and **find a local support group for single parents** – most areas have them and they offer the perfect opportunity to meet up with others in similar circumstances.

HAVE REALISTIC EXPECTATIONS

Focus on the days when things go right – not the ones when everything seems to fall apart.

Set realistic goals as a family and work towards them together. Plan ahead for fun – whether it's a week's holiday or a day trip to the zoo. Most importantly, give your kids credit when they do things well and **allow yourself credit for looking after them alone** – and making such a good job of it.

CHAPTER 5

Health and Beauty

Sleep Lab

Most of us need between **seven and nine hours of sleep a night** to feel great – but, hands up, who gets it? What with kids' homework and activities, work deadlines and housework, it sometimes seems impossible to fit in enough time for shut-eye. But going to bed is not just another job to do – it's vital to help you feel good and function properly.

Those people who get less sleep than their body needs build up what experts call **'sleep debt'.** This debt accumulates over time and takes its toll, leading to mood swings and depression. It can also affect the part of the brain that improves memory and learning.

Even a little sleep debt can have serious effects. Researchers have found that **sleep loss mimics some of the effects of ageing,** suggesting that it may increase the severity of age-related diseases such as obesity, diabetes and hypertension. Research has shown that getting enough sleep makes people more alert, productive and consequently happier with life.

HOW TO ENSURE you feel like you've had EIGHT hours – even when you've only had THREE!

To be on top form and able to cope with everything life throws at you, **adequate sleep every night is essential.** If that's just not happening for you, the following tips and tricks should help improve your quality and quantity of sleep.

CREATE A SLEEP HAVEN

Keep your bedroom quiet, dark and comfortable. For many people, **even the slightest noise or light can disturb sleep** – like the ticking of a clock or the light from your laptop or TV. Use window blinds (shades) or blackout curtains – anything necessary to make your room the perfect environment for sleep. The ideal room temperature is moderate to cool – too hot will actually hamper your ability to drop off.

GET CHILDREN TO BED EARLY

However brief, you need time to wind down in the evening between putting children to bed and going to bed yourself. For older children, make sure they are in their rooms, if not asleep, by a designated hour. Babies and young children will deter the best-laid plans but try to regulate bedtimes as much as possible – **tough scheduling of bedtimes early on** will save you many years of difficulty and allow you to have some semblance of an adult life.

KEEP THE BED FOR SLEEP AND SEX

Avoid watching TV, eating and discussing emotional issues in bed. The bed should be used for sleep and sex only. If not, **you can end up associating the bed with distracting activities** that could make it difficult for you to fall asleep. If there are still things on your mind when you go to bed, write your concerns down on a piece of paper and put the paper in a different room. They'll still be there to deal with when you wake up, so there's no point in worrying about them all night.

CHILL OUT!

Stop anything that requires serious concentration or causes stress 30 minutes before bedtime. According to sleep experts, **the best sleep-inducing activities are the boring ones!** You need to do something that takes your mind off trying to get to sleep, but at the same time is dull enough not to stimulate the brain too much. Re-reading a favourite book or doing the ironing is ideal.

CUT CAFFEINE

Simply put, caffeine can keep you awake, and can **stay in your body longer than you might think** – up to 14 hours. So, if you drink a cup of coffee at noon and are still awake at midnight, this could be the reason. Cutting out caffeine at least four to six hours before bedtime can help you fall asleep easier. If you have already had too much caffeine, try eating some carbohydrates, like bread or crackers, to help reduce the effects.

BAN BOOZE

Alcohol may initially help you fall asleep, but as your body clears it from your system, it can also cause symptoms that disturb sleep – like nightmares, sweats and headaches. **Drink one glass of water for every alcoholic beverage consumed** to reduce these symptoms. And try not to drink anything at all after 8 pm to stop you needing to get up to use the toilet during the night.

EAT RIGHT, SLEEP TIGHT

Try not to go to bed hungry, but **avoid heavy meals before bedtime** as they can cause indigestion or acid reflux, in which the contents of the stomach travel back up the oesophagus. If you can't avoid a late-night meal (which can be the case if you have dinner with your partner after you've fed the children), doctors advise you to sleep on your left side. This is because your stomach is on the left side of the body and the oesophagus enters it from the right. Lying on your left means the oesophagus is higher than your stomach, keeping the stomach contents away from it and preventing reflux.

STOP SNORERS

If your children aren't disturbing your sleep, your partner may well be! If he's a snorer, try recommending that he sleeps on his side, uses nasal strips or cuts out alcohol. Having high blood pressure, being overweight or allergies could be contributory factors.

WORK OUT – BUT NOT TOO LATE

If your body is pleasantly fatigued from exercise you will sleep better. So finish any aerobic exercise at least two hours before you go to bed. **Regular exercise can help you get a good night's sleep.** The timing and intensity of exercise seems to play a key role in its effects on sleep. If you are the type of person who gets energized or becomes more alert after exercise, it may be best not to exercise in the evening.

KEEP TO REGULAR HOURS

Avoid napping in the day or having lie-ins at the weekend. If you've had a late night on Saturday, a Sunday morning sleep-in is not the answer, as this will disrupt your internal body clock even more. If you have children, a lie-in won't be an option anyway and your kids will keep you on schedule. Try to get up at the same time as you do during the week, then have an early night on Sunday evening. This should get your sleep pattern back to normal and help you avoid feeling dreadful on Monday morning.

STILL CAN'T SLEEP?

Don't stress yourself out if you think you are not getting enough sleep. It will just make matters worse. Know you will sleep eventually. If you can't get to sleep for over 30 minutes, **get out of bed and do something boring** in dim light until you feel sleepy.

SNACKS to Help You Sleep

Many foods contain compounds that have a relaxing effect on the brain. So eating the right things before you go to bed will help get you in the mood for sleep. Scientists believe that **natural sedatives work by stimulating the brain to produce calming chemicals,** which promote a feeling of drowsiness.

> If you have trouble dropping off to sleep, eat one of these snooze-inducing snacks 40 minutes before bedtime to encourage a good night's rest.

HONEY WITH OATCAKES

To make

Simply spread two oatcakes with plenty of pure honey.

Why it works

Because of its high sugar content, honey is a soporific. It **boosts serotonin levels** and induces feelings of tranquillity. If falling asleep is a problem, eating honey before going to bed can really help. In fact, nutritional researcher Dr Judith Wurtman believes it can be as effective as a sleeping pill, but without the side-effect of grogginess in the morning. Also, the oatcakes are full of carbohydrates that stimulate the body to produce more of the hormone responsible for making us feel sleepy after a meal.

FRESH STRAWBERRY AND PINEAPPLE MILKSHAKE

To make

Chop and hull ten strawberries and trim and chop two large slices of fresh pineapple. Blend with 300 ml (1/2 pint) of semi-skimmed milk.

Why it works

Milk contains **natural opiates** (substances that induce sleep) called casomorphins, which have the power to make you feel drowsy. Pineapple contains bromelide, an enzyme that aids digestion, which means food won't lie in your stomach and stop you sleeping.

Super Skincare

Sometimes beauty really is skin deep – **nothing beats a fresh, glowing, line-free complexion.** But as we get older and our hormones fluctuate, our skin can change. Stress, having a baby and the menopause can all trigger problems such as breakouts, pigmentation and dryness.

The secret to a glowing complexion is to try and stick to a healthy, balanced diet, drink plenty of water, take time to pamper yourself to reduce stress and to choose the right products to care for your skin. The importance of careful cleansing and protection of your skin can't be underestimated. **Look after your skin well and you can keep any troublespots under control.**

Of course our skin will age, but thanks to some amazing developments in cosmetic procedures and skincare products, **you can help slow down this process.**

How to look after your skin AS YOU GET OLDER

YOUR 30s

This is the decade when skin may **start to lose some of its youthful bloom,** as cell turnover slows. Smoke, alcohol, pollution and UV light all cause premature ageing, and overexposure to any of them during your 20s will now begin to take its toll in the form of fine lines around your eyes and mouth. Collagen and elastin get weaker and wrinkles start to form as 'expression' lines. Skin looks generally duller than before and probably takes longer to recover from late nights or stress.

What you can do:

- Use SPF25 daily and wear a hat, or stay in the shade.

- Change to a richer moisturizer.

- To help brighten skin, slough off dead cells using a product containing alpha-hydroxy acids (AHAs).

- Don't wear heavy make-up. Choose cream-to-powder eye shadows, cheek and lip stains, and matt lipsticks.

YOUR 40s

The rate at which your skin renews itself really slows down in your 40s. Any signs of tiredness shows immediately in your face and thread veins may become more obvious. Your circulation and lymphatic drainage systems slow down too, which may cause puffiness around your eyes. **Hormones, however, play the biggest role around the time of the menopause,** and the drop in oestrogen can make skin thin and dry.

What you can do:

- Use SPF25 to protect skin from the sun and prevent any further cell damage from occurring.

- Treat yourself to monthly facials to keep skin in good condition.

- Use a cream containing retinol to exfoliate and reduce fine lines.

- Avoid dark lip and eye make-up as these accentuate lines. Go for peaches, pinks and beiges instead and try a light-reflecting micro-mineral foundation.

YOUR 50s

If you haven't protected your skin, sun damage will now be apparent in the form of wrinkles, spider veins and patches of pigmentation. You may notice **an apparent increase in the size of your pores.** They haven't actually got larger; the skin around them simply thickens with age and makes them look more pronounced. Decreased oestrogen levels slows sebum production, making skin drier.

What you can do:

- See a skin specialist to determine your skin's needs – you will find these to be very different from the past three decades.

- Apply a rich moisturizer containing SPF25, as continued protection from the sun will prevent further damage.

- If you choose to relax wrinkles using Botox, make sure you see an experienced doctor as side effects can include a droopy eye.

- Your make-up should gently enhance your features. Go for a light-reflective base and pale lip colours. Avoid powder eye shadows as they sit in the wrinkles and accentuate them.

The five SKINCARE SECRETS experts follow

1 **They get regular face treatments.** All skin needs a little pampering from time to time but experts know that a facial a month keeps skin in great condition.

2 **They spend money on their eyes.** Skin experts slather on eye cream. The skin around the eyes is very thin and therefore prone to early wrinkles. A little dab of eye cream can prevent and even reduce fine lines.

3 **They use the right cleanser.** For oily, acne-prone skin, try a gel containing salicylic acid. If you have dry, sensitive skin, you need a creamy or milky cleanser with calming ingredients like chamomile or aloe.

4 **They stay out of the sun.** Wear a hat, slather on high factor sunscreen every day and never go on sunbeds.

5 **They don't over-exfoliate.** As much as we like to help our skin along by scrubbing out all its impurities, the simple truth is some oils are necessary to act as a barrier. Stick to once a week to avoid irritation.

Adult Acne

The latest epidemic to hit stressed-out women is acne. Dermatologists are reporting an all-time high in 30–40 year-old women suffering from a serious pimple problem.

Teenage acne sufferers used to console themselves with the thought that they would eventually grow out of their spots, but **many older women are experiencing acne for the first time in their lives.** Acne sufferers have an increased sensitivity in their sebaceous (oil-producing) glands to normal levels of the male hormone testosterone. The cells that line the hair follicle become sticky and instead of being shed in the normal way, progressively block the duct so that oil and dead skin cannot escape. Bacteria then multiply around the blockage, causing inflammation, which results in red spots.

In the case of late-onset acne, **one of the main causes is thought to be stress,** which increases the production of male hormone. Diet may play some part in exacerbating the problem – studies have linked an excess of sugary carbohydrates to a worsening of acne – but it is not thought to be an actual cause. Neither is poor skincare – in fact, over-cleansing strips the skin of too much oil, making it produce more

and causing more spots. A gentle cleanser is best, along with an oil-free moisturizer to help keep skin line-free.

How to BEAT IT

The first-line treatment for mild-to-moderate acne is usually a topical cream or gel containing benzyl peroxide, but this can leave skin sore and red.

Oral antibiotics and certain contraceptive pills such as Dianette may be prescribed by your doctor. **The most powerful drug available is Roaccutane,** which has revolutionized the treatment of the condition. It is highly effective but has some unpleasant side-effects, such as liver problems, depression and skin dryness, and can only be prescribed through a dermatologist. It can also cause severe birth defects. The very latest treatment for acne is a laser treatment known as 'N-lite' that acts by killing the bacteria in the skin. It seems to work well for acne that is very red and inflamed. If your acne persists, look at trying to reduce your stress levels.

Making Time for You

Short-temperedness, frustration and feeling tearful can all be signs that you haven't left enough time in your schedule for you to unwind and relax, and you may even be feeling the effects of a build-up of resentment combined with exhaustion from sleep deprivation.

Premenstrual mood-swings are normal, but keep an eye on mood fluctuations that seem persistent or unusual. Getting some 'me time' is essential for everyone's mental health, and even more so for those with the added responsibility of caring for a family. You need to **look after your needs to keep you centred and strong enough to meet the demands of your lifestyle.** Here are some ways to reinvigorate your outlook and snatch some time for yourself in a busy schedule.

QUIET MORNING

Mornings can be hectic and full of activity. **Get a head start by waking up a good 15–20 minutes before your usual time** to have an early coffee and read a book, meditate or do a few stretching exercises. Make a real effort not to do anything remotely domestic until the other family members start to stir.

GRAB A NAP

A 15-minute snooze late afternoon **can do wonders for re-energizing you.** A short nap right before you need to pick the children up at school will give you a boost of energy to carry you through the evening ahead. If you work all week and this isn't possible, try sneaking in a nap on a Saturday or Sunday afternoon instead.

GET A FRESH OUTLOOK

If you feel as though you are stagnating in the daily routine of life, or hemmed in by a mountain of responsibilities, take some time to get away from the everyday by **trying something completely new.** It could be as simple as an exercise class you've never taken, a lecture you attend or an exhibition you visit, or as adventurous as a parachute jump or a trekking holiday. Even just a small, new activity will wake up your brain and make you feel you are living life rather than just treading water.

A DAY AT **THE SPA**

Finding time to fit in a facial, haircut, massage or manicure can be an impossible task. To avoid the feeling of disappointment when you can't get to regular appointments, book a day at a spa or salon once a month for head-to-toe treatments. **Look at it as a mini vacation** and you will feel like you've had a well-deserved break from the world.

Speedy Beauty Solutions

Sometimes getting enough time to brush your hair, let alone apply a full face of make-up, can be a challenge. But after your late 20s, going barefaced just isn't an option. **You need to look perfectly groomed at all times** – but in the shortest possible time.

Streamline your BEAUTY BAG

Here's how to adopt a minimalist approach to cosmetics by carefully streamlining your beauty kit down to the ten key products you really need.

1 Foundation

Choose a medium coverage product that suits your skin type. Some beauty companies will mix your shade for you personally to create the perfect colour. It costs a little more but is well worth the expense. And remember, you don't have to wear foundation all over your face every day. Only use what you need and if your skin looks good, save time and skip it.

2 Concealer

Buy a colour one shade lighter than your skin and use with a clean lipstick brush to cover dark shadows, spots and other imperfections in a jiffy. Some compacts contain two colours that you can mix together for the perfect skin match.

3 Powder

Loose is best if you're at home as it gives the most natural finish and is easy to apply. It is worth investing in one of those great little books of powdered papers to keep in your bag for daytime touch-ups.

4 Eyebrow pencil

Choose the same shade as your brows and use to fill in or define when needed.

5 Eyeliner

Choose a soft-textured pencil that can be applied easily and quickly.

6 Eyeshadow

Have one everyday colour and one shimmery signature shade for evenings. Forget elaborate shading techniques – they look very dated these days and take far too long. Stick to one or two shade combinations to keep it simple and fresh-looking.

7 Blusher

The right shade will make you look younger and healthier. Cream and gel blushes are the fastest and easiest to apply. Pop one blob in on the 'apple' or round part of each cheek and blend with your fingers.

8 Lip pencil

Save for evenings out, as applying it is too time-consuming for everyday make-up. Always blend to avoid that old-fashioned hard lip look. If you do suffer from a 'bleeding' lipline, use a sealing balm or primer before your lips – it will prevent the bleed without the hard edge of lipliner.

9 Lipstick

Forget fiddling around with brushes, using lipstick straight from the tube is easier and just as effective. Make sure you have one neutral shade and one more daring evening colour.

10 Mascara

Wear this cosmetic every day for eye definition and longer lashes. Choose lengthening formulations that are also waterproof, so you don't need to worry about re-applying or under-eye smudging during the day.

Desperate MEASURES

You're late for the nursery school drop-off and neither you nor babe are dressed. Don't panic: here's how to pull off 'naturally fabulous' in just a few minutes.

1 Forget the shower but freshen up with a couple of baby wipes, a squirt of deodorant and scent.

2 If your nail polish is chipped, simply remove with some quick-fix wipes and go nude – but give them a quick scrub. Dirty fingernails are a real no-no.

3 No time to brush your teeth? Simply chew gum or crunch a couple of mints for instantly fresher breath.

4 Slap a bit of moisturizer onto your face and hands.

5 Give your face a quick touch-up. Apply a radiance booster, cover any dark circles or spots with concealer. Then use a multipurpose stick colour for the cheeks, eyes and lips, then finish with one quick coat of mascara.

6 Pull dirty hair off your face in a classic chignon or with an Alice band – this will make you look fresh-faced and clean – even if you don't feel it!

Beat the Age Trap

Although ageing is sadly inevitable, showing the signs of it doesn't have to be. Most of what we think of as the visible signs of ageing are actually the **accumulated effects of lifestyle factors** such as smoking, too much sunshine, a poor diet and stress. And these days you'll find a whole arsenal of age-erasers at your nearest beauty counter to help undo some of the damage.

Here's how to **slow down the ageing process** and delay that facelift...

USE SUNSCREEN

In the morning, before you leave for work, **apply a sunscreen, SPF 25 or higher, or a make-up base with UV protection.** You could also use a moisturizer containing sunscreen as well. This routine, over many years, will make a big difference to how your skin ages.

WEAR SUNGLASSES

You won't squint as much. Over time, a lot of squinting will lead to lines and wrinkles. Choose styles extending over the sides of the face to help shield crow's feet. And don't forget your hat, either.

STAY OFF THAT SUNBED

There's no such thing as a safe tan unless it comes in a bottle. In fact, some experts feel tanning beds are more dangerous because some of them have a higher concentration of UVA rays. UVA penetrates deeper into the skin, and we don't know what the longer-term results of that deeper penetration are. We do know that it ages the skin, however.

USE THE RIGHT
ANTI-AGEING
PRODUCTS

If you're using a moisturizer with alpha hydroxy, be sure to **get one with enough of the acid in it.** Typically, you're looking for something with ten per cent glycolic or alpha-hydroxy acid for it to be effective. Some cosmetics boast of Vitamin C or its derivatives for their antioxidant effects. While it is true that vitamin C is a potent antioxidant, a lot of those topical products don't penetrate into the skin. If you are going to spend money on a product, make sure you check their claims carefully.

GET INTO A
NIGHT-TIME
RITUAL

In the evening you have more time to devote to skin maintenance, so try to make it a habit. Your skincare programme should **include a retinol-based skincare product after cleansing,** to keep the outer dead layers of the skin peeled away and to hydrate the deeper layers.

DON'T
SMOKE

Smoking breaks down the natural proteins in the skin – the collagen and the elastin. It also decreases the blood supply to the skin and causes puckering lines to form permanently around the mouth.

Eat Yourself Younger

It's not only what you put on your skin that can help prevent wrinkles, **what you put into your mouth is just as important.** While good skincare, plenty of sleep and avoiding too much sun all help beat the age trap, following a good diet is also essential.

No amount of expensive lotions and potions will help stave off the ravages of time unless you're eating the right anti-ageing foods, which research suggests **are mainly brightly coloured fruit and vegetables, fish and – believe it or not – chocolate.** This is because they are packed with chemicals called antioxidants, which help fight off 'free radical' damage, which attacks the body's cells and triggers premature ageing.

EIGHT ANTI-AGEING superfoods

1 Apples

This fruit is anti-ageing because it is one of the richest food sources of flavonols – **powerful antioxidants** that can protect the skin cells from the damaging chemicals in the environment.

2 Berries

Purple, dark red and blue berries, and dark cherries, are all anti-ageing because they get their colour from the antioxidant flavonoid anthocyanin. Studies show this can **help strengthen the walls of small blood vessels,** helping prevent unsightly thread veins that occur with age.

3 Brazil nuts

The richest food source of selenium, an antioxidant enzyme that neutralizes free radicals and is **regarded as an anti-cancer agent.**

4 Leafy green vegetables

Vegetables such as broccoli and spinach are anti-ageing because they contain a variety of phytochemicals that help **stimulate the production of enzymes** of the body's natural defence system, which detoxifies cancer-causing and ageing chemicals in the body.

5 Chocolate

Oh yes! People who eat it regularly **live on average one extra year.** This is due to phenols (a type of antioxidant) found in every woman's favourite treat.

6 Kiwi fruit

Contains **twice the vitamin C of oranges** and as much vitamin E as avocados – both of which are powerful anti-ageing nutrients.

7 Oily fish

Mackerel, sardines, salmon and trout are some of the richest sources of **protective omega-3 fatty acids.** You need to eat two oily fish meals a week to appreciate their anti-ageing benefits.

8 Soya foods and soya milk

Anti-ageing because they contain isoflavones. These plant hormones are physically identical to the female sex hormone oestradiol made by the ovaries and adrenal glands. They **help protect against heart disease and osteoporosis, and beat menopause symptoms.**

Family Nutrition

Beware the pitfalls of preparing meals for the family. From making sandwiches for kids' lunches at 6 am until the end of the day when you're often cooking two evening meals – an early one for hungry children and a later one for your partner – **you're having to think about other people's food needs all day and every day.**

And although it's unlikely you are able to cut down on the number of meals you have to prepare, you can get disciplined about how you approach food. Like it or not, **your attitudes toward food will shape those of your family.**

EAT TOGETHER

Make an effort to sit down together at the table once a day – preferably for the evening meal. This allows the meal to have a **specific beginning and end,** preventing it from extending all evening as family members come in from activities or work to eat at various times. It will also limit your time in the kitchen and prevent the family from overeating.

HEALTHY ALTERNATIVES

Make **home-made versions of junk-food** favourites, such as burgers, chips and pizza. Serve a grilled burger with a salad instead of a bun, top a wholemeal pizza base with vegetables and use minimal cheese, or brush potato chunks with a little olive oil and bake them instead of deep frying.

ENLIST HELP
IN THE KITCHEN

Asking your children and partner to help plan and prepare meals will make your tasks easier and also provide an opportunity for them to **learn about good nutrition.**

YOU CAN'T EAT
WHAT YOU DON'T BUY

Don't shop for food when you are hungry, as you'll be more tempted to buy less nutritional ingredients. If the food is not in the home, you can't eat it. You are probably the main shopper in the family so **it's up to you to set the tone.** If children scream for treats, let them choose between two good choices – giving them an option will make them think they are in control.

AVOID READY MEALS

At some point everyone relies on a quick meal, but most prepared meals from supermarkets contain many more calories, salt and sugar than similar versions made from fresh ingredients at home. **Try to make a couple of big batches of one-pot meals** over the weekend and freeze them to use in the weeks to come.

RESTAURANT EATING

Share and share alike. Children's restaurant meals are notoriously unhealthy. To remedy this, **split an adult-sized meal with your child and get a salad or extra side vegetables.** Sharing a dessert two or four ways means that everyone gets a taste without the full calorific effect.

Diet Dilemmas

There are diets for all personalities and lifestyles, but **following a specific programme can be tough.** You may find you are cooking more meals or buying different ingredients to fulfil your diet and your family's, or that you are under increased temptation while you cook.

The most practical and longlasting alternative, however, is to simply modify your everyday eating plans, opting for smaller quantities, grilling rather than frying, and limiting rich foods and sauces. Just by setting some new nutritional guidelines you may be able to **shed pounds almost without effort.**

Five ways to stop being a SLAVE TO THE SCALES

1 DON'T CLEAN YOUR PLATE

As your body gets older, it burns calories less efficiently, so although you may be following the same diet that kept you slim at 20, it no longer works when you're 40. Cutting just 100 calories – the equivalent of **leaving just two bites** on your plate – will combat this.

2 THINK BEFORE YOU DRINK

Studies show that your body doesn't register a feeling of fullness from the calories you drink. This is why **liquid calories help you gain weight** by causing you to overeat later. So, next time you fancy a drink have a big glass of water and a healthy snack.

3 NUMBER OBSESSED

Your weight fluctuates from day to day, even morning to afternoon so don't live or die by what the scales say. It's better to **judge whether you need to lose a few pounds by seeing how your clothes fit.** If they're too tight, don't bite!

4 MAKE STAYING IN SHAPE A HABIT

Finding time to exercise only gets harder as you get older. It helps to remember that working out gives you the sanity, strength and good health to keep the rest of your world running smoothly. Committing to a fitness routine will make you feel better inside and out.

5 SLASH STRESS

Some days just managing to make it to midnight without a major drama is an accomplishment in itself. **Stress is one of the biggest reasons why women overeat,** so taking a few minutes each day to unwind is key to your weight-loss success. Soak in a hot bath, play some music or do a yoga class – whatever it takes to bring that blood pressure down!

Ten Ways to Look Ten Years Younger

1 *Get quality sleep*
At least eight hours every night will make you look years younger. Go to bed as early as possible – and try to make sure it's before midnight.

2 *Be a long, tall Sally*
Recapture the figure of your youth by using visual tricks to produce long, lean lines. Slim-fit jeans or trousers with a boot-cut leg, topped with a fitted, but not skintight top and finished off with high heels will do the job perfectly.

3 *Don't over-diet or over-exercise*
This makes you appear scrawny and gaunt. Rounder faces appear younger and the wrinkles fill out a bit. A bit of exercise gets the blood flowing, and reminds your muscles they exist. Too much intense exercise, especially outdoor running, can make you look haggard.

4 *Straighten up*
By the time we hit our 30s, most of us have been slouching for so long that we don't even realize we're doing it. Slouching can make you look – and feel – older than you are. For great posture, keep your head level and pull your chin straight back.

5 *Go glossy*
Keep your hair in great condition. Shiny hair is youthful and one of the most effective ways to turn back the clock. And while you're focusing on your hair, be sure to always have a modern cut. There is nothing more ageing than a woman with a stiff, dated hairdo. Try to rethink your hairstyle, with the help of a good stylist, at least every two to three years.

6 Get groomed

Our brows, like the hair on our head, get thinner with age. Filling in sparse brows and extending them works to lift the eyes and frame the face. When time counts, a brow powder gets the job done more subtly and quickly than a pencil – just a few strokes will make a big difference.

7 Maintain white teeth

Yellow, discoloured teeth instantly put years on your face. It's so easy and inexpensive to whiten teeth at home now, or for more dramatic results ask your dentist about in-house whitening treatments.

8 Guzzle water

Be a juicy plum instead of a dried prune. Drink eight to ten glasses of water a day instead of coffee and tea. Caffeine sucks water out of your body and makes your skin look and feel like scrunched-up paper.

9 Stop worrying

If you have problems, resolve to deal with them and then put them out of your mind. Stress and worry make you haggard, and predispose you to disease. They keep you awake at night, and ruin the quality of your sleep.

10 Have sex

Making love three times a week can make you look ten years younger, according to Scottish research. A vigorous sex life was found to be the second most important determinant of how young a person looked. Only formal exercise proved more important than sex in keeping ageing at bay.

How to Hold Back the Hands of Time

These days it seems as though **everyone's at it.** A nip and tuck here, a filler or touch of Botox there. Once the sole preserve of the rich and famous, cosmetic surgery has become commonplace among us ordinary folk.

Minimally invasive approaches such as collagen and Botox are also hugely popular ways to reverse the ravages of time. The same holds true for laser resurfacing and chemical peels. But invasive surgical procedures, such as eye lifts or facelifts, are also seen as pretty normal today.

There will always be pressure to look good, but choosing whether or not to have surgery is a personal choice. Beauty is subjective and how you see yourself is what counts, so learning to make the most of what you've got is important. But if something about your appearance really bothers you, **take steps to improve upon it – within reason.** While a good cosmetic or plastic surgeon can make an incredible difference to your appearance, too much of a good thing can look unnatural or even downright bizarre. A little wrinkle here and there that shows a face full of life is far more attractive than having a permanent look of surprise.

If you do choose to have any kind of work done, make sure you check the surgeon's credentials. As in any medical procedure, **there is a certain amount of risk involved and often a big price tag.** The good news is techniques have been refined over the last ten years, which means surgery, when performed by an experienced doctor, is now safer than ever and the results are better, too.

Nonsurgical or THE KNIFE?

There are areas you can fix without plastic surgery.
You'd be surprised by how much better problem spots
like the following can look if you work at them with
cosmetics, or non-surgical procedures like lasers, chemical
peels, Botox or fillers.

- Dark under-eye circles
- Discolouration or pigmentation
- Lines – e.g. at the corners of the mouth
- Vertical frown lines between eyebrows
- Lines above the upper lip
- Fine wrinkles on the cheeks
- Fine wrinkles under the eyes
- Smile lines around the eyes
- Dry or blotchy skin
- Oily, irregular skin
- Slight fullness along the jawline
- Double chin

Don't believe the hype. For the following problems you'll
either have to learn to love them or opt for surgery.

- Excess eyelid skin
- Puffiness or deep under-eye circles
- Deep frown lines between eyebrows
- Jowls hanging over the jawline
- Hanging skin and deep facial wrinkles
- Very loose neck skin
- Loss of cheek fullness

Tackle those TROUBLE SPOTS

When most of us wake up and look in the mirror, we feel reasonably happy with what we see. Until we look a bit closer that is, and start to notice **the furrowed brow** that stays even when you're not frowning; or **those dark circles that never go,** however much sleep you get. And while we're on the subject, wouldn't it be nice if your chin wasn't quite so saggy?

Don't worry, **help is at hand**. Try some of these tricks to combat those tell-tale signs of ageing and keep you looking as young as you feel.

BANISH YOUR EYEBAGS

What causes it?

Blood vessels showing underneath skin and or skin that's hyperpigmented – become darker – due to sun exposure.

Do-it-yourself fix

Retinol, the form of topical vitamin A found in over-the-counter products, helps under-eye circles in two ways: first by fading melanin, the skin pigment that often contributes to darkness; and second by stimulating production of collagen – the substance that keeps skin plump. Expect to see some improvement within three to six months.

The surgical solution

The V-beam, a state-of-the-art laser that seals the blood vessels below the skin without damaging the skin itself.

KEEP YOUR
CHIN UP

What causes it

Jowls and a double chin are a result of genetics, gravity, sun damage and a redistribution of the underlying fat around the jaw line.

Do-it-yourself fix

Firming creams. These products have no permanent effect on the skin, but they can create tighter contours by firming up the superficial layer of the skin.

The surgical solution

Liposuction. Yes, it's pricey, but surgery is the only permanent solution – and now it's a simple, fairly low-risk procedure. Before signing up, make sure the surgeon is registered and has performed the surgery at least 100 times.

FORGET THOSE
FROWN LINES

What causes it?

With repeated contractions of the muscles responsible for frowning, furrows become etched into your brow.

Do-it-yourself fix

Frownies are a well-kept celebrity wrinkle-busting secret. These adhesive patches are applied to your forehead to smooth and relax muscles while you sleep. Or try one of the new wave of topical creams that call themselves 'Botox in a jar'. Most contain an ingredient that reduces your muscles' ability to contract. It takes up to two months to see the full effect – a slight, but hopefully noticeable decrease in your ability to frown.

The surgical solution

Botox, a highly purified form of the toxin that causes botulism, administered with a needle. Don't let the word 'botulism' scare you – the amount used is very small and thus harmless. When injected in low doses, Botox paralyzes muscles so they can't contract and cause expression lines, such as forehead wrinkles and crow's feet. Results, which can take a week to kick in, can last for up to six months.

TAKE TIME OFF
YOUR HANDS

What causes it?

Liver spots on the backs of your hands are caused by years of exposure to the sun.

Do-it-yourself fix

A three-pronged approach that includes daily use of **lightening products, exfoliators and high SPF sunscreen.**

The surgical solution

A cosmetic surgeon will use the same idea but with stronger products – **chemical peels and pigment-zapping lasers** – for a more pronounced effect.

DE-AGE YOUR
DÉCOLLETAGE

What causes it?

Splotching and crinkling on the chest are the markings of sun exposure.

Do-it-yourself fix

Look for **creams formulated with kinetin,** a plant-based growth hormone that softens fine lines and clears brown spots. It's non-irritating, which makes it ideal for this sensitive and fragile skin. You should notice an improvement after four to six weeks.

The surgical solution

Lasers significantly lighten melanin, the skin pigment that clumps together to cause mottling. **Light chemical peels** with agents such as glycolic acid and salicylic acid can help smooth fine lines and fade brown spots, but you will need several sessions depending on how serious the sun damage is.

Get LIPPY

Lips are one of the **key areas that can give away your age.** Try the following tips for a fuller, softer, younger-looking mouth that will soon give you something to smile about.

STOP
FEATHERING

As the skin around your lips wrinkles, lips look puckered and lipstick can bleed into the lines.

Fast fix

Lip liner creates a barrier that keeps the colour exactly where you want it. Another trick is to lightly dust face powder above lips to keep the area dry, as any moisture there will encourage feathering.

Lasting solution

A cosmetic surgeon can give **filler injections** to plump out lines above lips. These last for up to six months.

BEAT
THINNING

Loss of collagen and fat over time means less plumpness.

Fast fix

Tinted balms or lip plumping products can create the pouty effect of gloss without looking too young. Or, to make your lips look thicker, apply foundation just beyond your mouth's outer edges, then cover lips and the foundation area with lipstick.

Lasting solution

Fillers add fullness, but avoid silicone as it can create permanent, unsightly bumps. A better option is to try above-the-lip injections, which redefine the mouth in a more natural way.

SMOOTH
CHAPPING

Skin loses moisture as you age, which means drier, flakier lips.

Fast fix

A lip exfoliant with gentle scrubbers will remove flakes fast. Follow with some Vaseline or lip balm.

Lasting solution

When your lips thin out, their surface wrinkles up, making them look even drier. Over time, the ingredient **retinol** can help soften and smooth creases. Since lip skin is thin and easily irritated, use a product made just for lips. Apply just before bed.

Hair Concerns

There's no getting away from the fact that the older we get, the more our hair needs looking after. As a teen it was easy to get away with an unkempt look, but once past 30, **your hair needs to reflect your age, confidence and status.**

It needs to be soft, shiny and in great shape. Here are some ways to maintain your crowning glory.

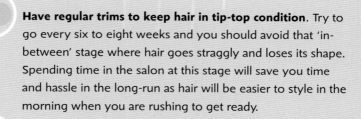 **Have regular trims to keep hair in tip-top condition**. Try to go every six to eight weeks and you should avoid that 'in-between' stage where hair goes straggly and loses its shape. Spending time in the salon at this stage will save you time and hassle in the long-run as hair will be easier to style in the morning when you are rushing to get ready.

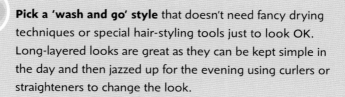 **Pick a 'wash and go' style** that doesn't need fancy drying techniques or special hair-styling tools just to look OK. Long-layered looks are great as they can be kept simple in the day and then jazzed up for the evening using curlers or straighteners to change the look.

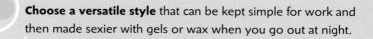 **Choose a versatile style** that can be kept simple for work and then made sexier with gels or wax when you go out at night.

Use a deep moisture treatment, whatever your hair type. Applied once a week it will replenish and protect your hair, and help keep it shiny.

Ask your hairdresser to give you a blow-drying lesson – many salons offer them now. He can show you some of the tricks of the trade so you can create salon-looking hair without leaving your house.

STYLE CLINIC – pick the right style, whatever your age

Your 30s

Women at this age are usually busy settling into careers or motherhood – or both. **At this age, we want to prove ourselves and be taken seriously.** Go for hairstyles that are classic yet versatile and need little blow-drying to look good.

Your 40s

This tends to be the age where **most women go short,** because long hair tends to pull the face down. However, trends are changing and women are wearing their hair long well into their 40s. The trick is to avoid extremes: you don't want to go too long or try out a colour or cut that's simply too young. If you do decide on staying longer, have plenty of layers, especially around the face.

Your 50s

By the time we hit our 50s, there's nothing to prove. After a lifetime of caring for others, worrying about what they think, we come into our own and do things for ourselves. **It's a great time to rediscover your fun and flirty side** – or be bold and go super short.

How to Blitz those Body Blackspots

Can you remember when no part of your body sagged, drooped or wobbled? **What goes wrong when we hit mid-life?** Unfortunately, science works against us – the greatest physical decline in the human body occurs during the decade between 30 and 40 years of age.

During this decade muscle mass is lost, the metabolism slows down, bones lose density, flexibility and strength declines and body fat increases. In fact, the average woman gains approximately 9 kg (20 lb) between the ages of 20 and 65. This **physical decline is partly due to the metabolism slow down** that creeps up, but it is also largely down to inactivity.

BINGO **WINGS**

Unless a woman is working out two to three times a week, by the time she hits her 40s **the muscles in the backs of her arms may be headed south.** To tone up flabby underarms, try the arm-strengthening yoga pose below.

How to do it

Sit on the floor with your legs out in front and drawn together. Keep your back straight and place your palms on the floor behind you, fingertips pointing away. Pressing down, lean back onto your hands and lift your hips and the whole front of your body toward the ceiling. Imagine your thighs are being pulled up by invisible strings. Keep your arms and legs straight and point your toes away from your body. Look straight ahead and hold for ten seconds before releasing back down to the floor. Repeat five times a day, every day, to see results.

Note: Check with your doctor before doing this move
if you're pregnant or have any neck or back injuries.

SAGGY **BOOBS**

It's a sad fact of life that our breasts can't stay perky for ever and gravity always wins in the end. But **exercise can help keep them as pert as possible.** Although breasts themselves are made up of fatty tissue, lifting weights will firm the pectoral muscles that support them, for great uplift.

How to do it

Use light weights of 2 kg (5 lb) to tone without bulk.

Hold one weight in each hand by your sides, then raise both to shoulder level, keeping your arms out at the sides. Do three sets of ten to 15, repeat both moves every other day for fast results.

WOBBLY BUM

Unfortunately, even when we're in a job that stimulates the mind, **our bottom muscles are bored** by up to eight hours of daily inactivity. Your workouts should include all forms of cardiovascular training, but especially activities that target the gluteal region, like step classes, brisk walking, skipping and running. But dumbbell squats are the way to get a gravity-defying bum – fast.

How to do it

You'll need a good pair of dumbbells that weigh 5 kg (10 lb) each. Stand straight with your feet slightly apart. Hold a dumbbell in each hand, keeping your arms by your sides, palms in. Looking straight ahead, inhale and lower your body as if you're sitting back into a chair until your thighs are as parallel to the floor as possible. Return to your starting position, exhaling as you go.

To see results, you'll need to squeeze in two to three sets of 15 squats, three times a week. After three weeks you'll start to notice a definite improvement.

LOVE HANDLES AND/OR **POT BELLY**

The dreaded middle-age spread can take the form of a sticking-out tummy or generous love handles that flop not so lovingly over your favourite jeans. **A natural side-effect of ageing,** only losing weight and exercise will shift it. Try running for ten minutes on a treadmill every day. This will boost your metabolism so you burn more fat and calories. But it's sit-ups that will really flatten the abs, both at the front of the stomach and at the sides.

How to do it

To target those jelly bellies, it's crunch time. Crunches really are the best way to flatten the six-pack area, so aim for five sets of 20.

Bicycle twists will really help the love handles. This is where you bring your left leg in to meet your right elbow (and vice versa) as you do sit-ups. Doing this tones the muscles at the sides of your stomach known as the obliques. Aim for three sets of 20 and repeat every other day for great results.

FLABBY LEGS

Maybe we walk around more when we're young, but for some reason, **once we hit our 30s our legs get chunkier.** If you want long, lean, defined legs, any form of cardiovascular training done slowly but steadily three to four times a week for at least 20 minutes will have positive results. These activities can include brisk walking, taking a dance class or kickboxing.

To really sculpt those calf muscles, try plié squats.

How to do it
Stand with your feet a little more than shoulder-width apart, toes pointed out. Raise yourself up on to your toes and, keeping your back straight, abs tight and butt tucked in, bend down from the knees until your thighs are parallel to the ground. Do three sets of 20 every other day for top results.

Beat Cellulite for Good

We all have it and we all want to get rid of it. I'm talking about cellulite – the unsightly orange peel skin that forms on a woman's bottom and thighs. Fortunately, we can do something about it.

Cellulite is a mixture of fat, fluid and toxins trapped within the connective tissues of the skin. **The hormone oestrogen makes women collect fat around their bottom and thighs,** and if you think of fat cells as being stored in lots of little boxes made from collagen, women's fat boxes are weaker than men's. And that means fat often bulges out of them. Couple this with poor-functioning circulatory systems brought on by bad diet, lack of exercise, the pill, ageing, genetics and hey presto, you've a recipe for disaster.

The FOUR STAGES of cellulite

STAGE 1

How it looks:

At this stage cellulite is still quite firm and you probably only notice it when you squidge the area between your fingers.

What it means:

Your fat cells have started to get bigger – perhaps you've put on weight – and are now holding more water and toxins, making them bulge.

Why you're likely to be a victim:

You're probably under 30 and on the pill, a smoker or... hard luck, it runs in the family.

How to combat it:

GET MOVING!

Exercise is important as it improves circulation, burns fat and helps you tone up – all vital for a smooth, firm bottom half. Do it with some friends to help make it into a social occasion – you can all commiserate together!

DITCH THE READY MEAL

Eating less processed foods and more fresh fruit and veg will reduce the toxin load on your body, so less is stored in the fat cells.

STAGE 2

How it looks:

Cellulite is more noticeable, but is still only in small areas. Skin may also be blotchy in these places.

What it means:

The collagen holding your fat cells together has started to weaken, giving your skin an uneven, bumpy appearance.

Why you're likely to be a victim:

This usually happens to woman between 30 and 35, but can occur at a younger age if you never exercise or follow a high-fat diet. Pregnancy can also make things worse, due to the increase in oestrogen levels.

How to combat it:

CUT DOWN ON CAFFEINE

Coffee, tea and chocolate are all packed with this stimulant, high doses of which will slow down lymph flow and its elimination of toxins. So while the odd cup won't hurt, if you're a five espressos-a-day girl, it may be time to discover the delights of herbal tea?

GIVE IT A RUB

Massaging your skin every day with cellulite-busting essential oils will boost circulation and reduce the appearance of lumpy skin.

STAGE 3

How it looks:

By now you have bigger areas of cellulite that are quite noticeable. Skin is saggy and blotchy all over.

What it means:

Circulation is severely restricted to the affected areas so fat cells have become very swollen with water, fat and toxins. Plus your collagen fibres have started to break down making skin less able to hold in the bulkier fat cells.

Why you're likely to be a victim:

This stage usually affects women between 35 and 40 who've had children, been on the pill or are overweight.

How to combat it:

UP YOUR EXERCISE LEVELS

The best anti-cellulite exercises are brisk walking, running or cycling, while moves like squats and lunges will tone your muscles and improve the look of lumpy skin. Try for at least 15 minutes of exercise every day. And yes, shagging counts – if you exert yourself enough that is. . .

BOOST YOUR DIGESTION

If you're often constipated it can make cellulite worse. When toxins don't pass out though the colon, they can slow down the efficiency of organs such as the liver. Increase your fibre intake with plenty of wholegrains, get at least five portions of fruit and veg every day and drink lots of water.

STAGE 4

How it looks:

The most advanced stage. Now lumps and bumps are so noticeable they can be spotted through clothing.

What it means:

Complete collagen breakdown means the fibres can no longer contain swollen fat cells, creating deeper dimples. Little blood reaches these areas, making them blotchy and clammy to touch.

Why you're likely to be a victim:

This stage usually affects women over 40 who've had children, although poor diet, obesity and lack of exercise can cause it to occur at a younger age.

How to combat it:

FAKE IT

It's official: cellulite looks heaps better when it's brown. So before you hit the beach, invest in a good fake tan or treat yourself to a professional spray treatment.

TRY TECHNOLOGY

Endermologie is the only cellulite treatment to be approved by the US Food and Drug Administration. A therapist uses a hand-held pump to suck and roll your flesh, flushing out toxins and encouraging excess fat to break down.

Take Fitness in Hand

The very time that many women fall off the exercise wagon is actually when it's most critical to stay on board. Think about it: do you drive where you used to walk? Sit at a desk for long hours when you used to be constantly on the run? Do you eat out more, go dancing less and always get a taxi home? **It's so easy to slip into habits of inactivity** especially when we're busy juggling different areas of life. Then we look in the mirror one day and wonder when it all went wrong. But even if you've reached that stage, it's not too late to regain fitness and improve your health.

Regular aerobic exercise can aid weight loss and reduce many health risks as well as providing time out from a hectic schedule.

While cardiovascular exercise is crucial for maintaining health and wellbeing, it's strength – or resistance training – that will make the biggest impact on your mid-life body shape. The basal metabolic rate – the rate at which we burn calories at rest – begins to decline from 25–30 years of age. By increasing lean body mass through exercise, this decline can be reversed. **The best way to achieve this is to work out two to three times a week.**

But if you're wondering how on earth you can fit yet another thing into your time-starved life, take heart. Studies increasingly show that **lifestyle activities are just as instrumental in keeping us fit and healthy** as formal exercise. In fact, one landmark study at the University of Maastricht found that people who were sedentary most of the day but went to the gym regularly burned fewer calories than those who were generally more active in their daily lives but didn't do any structured workouts.

EXERCISE from 30 onwards

30s

Without exercise, **your body's metabolic rate and muscle tone will start to decline,** so if you've never been one for the gym, now is the time to start! Ideally, you should combine aerobic exercise with some weight training to help build bone mass and protect against osteoporosis. You may notice a reduction in flexibility, so include stretching exercises to keep your body supple.

> **Good workout choices:** Yoga, Pilates, weight training, dancing and running.

40s

This is the period when you'll start to notice your body ageing, especially if you've been inactive during your 20s and 30s. But it's never too late to get fit. During your 40s, you should **shift the emphasis from energetic workouts to lower impact exercise** to minimize stress on the body. Try to include some gentle weight training too, as you need muscle to burn off calories and protect you from injury. Exercise also helps to ward off middle-age spread, which occurs when your metabolic rate slows down.

> **Good workout choices:** Yoga, Pilates, tennis, light weights and circuit training.

50s

If you've been active all your life, your body will thank you now as you'll be in much better shape than someone who's always been sedentary. But bear in mind loss of bone mass will make you more susceptible to fractures, so you need to be careful when you work out. **Try weight-bearing exercises** such as brisk walking. It's very important to stay active at this age, so don't change your two-up two-down for a single storey bungalow – it will make you lazy and you'll forget what stairs look like!

> **Good workout choices:** Brisk walking, yoga and swimming.

WARNING

If you haven't exercised for a long time, **start slowly.** Sports medicine professionals have coined the phrase 'boomeritis' to describe the wide variety of injuries they are seeing as a result of middle-aged people taking to exercise a little too energetically.

Health MOT

When you're caught up in day-to-day living, regular health checks can fall by the wayside. It's easy to think, 'I don't feel ill, so why should I go to the doctor?' The problem with this is that many illnesses can only be treated when caught early. So, **don't wait for symptoms,** make sure you have the screening tests you need. From mammograms to cholesterol tests, they couldn't be more crucial.

The VITAL HEALTH CHECKS every woman must have

From the AGE OF 20

CHOLESTEROL TEST

Even in your 20s, you should have been keeping an eye on your cholesterol levels. If it's normal, the test should be repeated every five years. High cholesterol is linked to an increased risk of heart disease, so it's important to find out if your levels are high. If they are, simple diet changes will help to bring them down.

CHECK YOUR OWN BREASTS

It's vital to check your breasts regularly for lumps or changes. Breast cancer is far easier to treat and has a higher survival rate when caught early. It's important to become familiar with how your breasts look and feel, and to know what is normal for them. Report any changes to your doctor without delay.

PAP TEST AND PELVIC EXAM

In a Pap test, doctors take cells from the cervix to look for early warning signs of cancer that cause no symptoms. A woman should get the test about three years after she first becomes sexually active, and no later than age 21. After that, she needs to be tested every two to three years.

STI TESTS

If you're sexually active, you should be screened for sexually transmitted infections. The most common of these is chlamydia, which, if left untreated, can lead to infertility. Other common nasties include gonorrhoea, syphilis, HIV, HPV (human papilloma virus) and herpes.

SKIN CANCER SCREENING

Every three months, it's a good idea to check your skin for anything suspicious, and to have your doctor look you over once a year for abnormal freckles, moles, lesions or nodules. This is more crucial if you've spent a lot of time in the sun or have a family history of skin cancer.

From the AGE OF 30

In your 30s you should have roughly the same tests and exams that you got in your 20s plus any discretionary tests ordered by your doctor, such as **a mammogram if you have a family history of breast cancer.**

BONE DENSITY TEST

At 35, you should also start paying attention to your bones, which means **getting enough calcium and doing weight-bearing exercise** such as power-walking. Most women don't require a bone-density exam for another 15 years, but those who are significantly underweight, who've had an eating disorder or who have a family history of osteoporosis may need the test earlier.

From the AGE OF 40

As well as the tests you should have in your 20s and 30s, after 40 you should also include the ones listed below. Even though the average age of menopause is 50, many women in their 40s also become apprehensive about the signs and symptoms of this upcoming hormonal shift.

BOWEL CANCER TESTS

Cancers of the colon and rectum are more prevalent as you get older. Stool checks can be used to detect any blood in faecal matter and a rectal exam or colonoscopy can be used to detect polyps or other irregularities that may be a sign of increased risk.

MAMMOGRAM AND BREAST EXAM

After the age of 50 you should have a yearly mammogram. However, if you have a history of breast cancer in your family your doctor may recommend you begin having mammograms from 35. This test can highlight cancerous tumours up to two years before a lump is large enough to be felt.

DIABETES TEST

Having Type 2 diabetes means that your blood sugar rises because you can't make enough insulin or use it properly. A lot of women get diabetes in middle age or older, but the rate is rising among younger women along due to the increase in obesity. To see if you're at risk, have a blood test to screen for it every three years. This is more vital if your blood pressure or cholesterol is high.

HEART DISEASE SCREENING

Obesity, high blood pressure, high-fat diets and diabetes fuel heart disease. Women often do not recognize their heart attack symptoms because they are more likely than men to experience indigestion, breathing trouble or muscle pain instead of the classic spreading chest pain. It is vital, therefore, to keep up regular cholesterol and blood pressure tests.

How Not to Grow Old Gracefully

You're only as old as you feel claim the experts. But if you're 40 and feel 60, then it's time for some action. **Age is a psychological as well as a physical state,** so if you look after your mind and your body together, it's possible to slow down the ageing process. Whatever your age, there are always new opportunities, experiences and ambitions to grab hold of and enjoy. So look forward to your next birthday instead of dreading it, embrace life and follow these tips to an older, wiser, newer feeling you.

GET **FIT**

Exercise wards off many ills and keeps you mentally and physically in good shape. It keeps the joints supple, the heart pumping and the adrenaline racing. So grab that tennis racket or bicycle, stick on some trainers and get going. **Join your local gym** and make a deal with a friend that for every class or workout you do, you'll have a beauty treatment in the spa or a relaxing session in the steam room.

THINK **YOURSELF YOUNG**

Learning a new skill or furthering an existing talent keeps your body and brain stimulated. Take an evening class, start a reading group or learn a new sport. The buzz of **doing something new and meeting new people will take years off you** – and create some precious 'me' time.

DRESS WELL

There's no point in dressing head-to-toe in the latest trends; you'll simply look like a fashion victim or as if you are trying too hard. By now you know what your best features are, so **build on your own unique style** and be confident that you look great – it takes years off you.

IT'S NEVER TOO LATE

If you're a banker but are desperate to be a singer, or have always wanted to travel around South America, or wanted to start your own business – **don't just think about it, do it!** Don't get stuck in a rut by thinking 'I'll do something different tomorrow' – reinvigorate your life and do it now.

LOOK TO THE FUTURE

Your 20s were the best years of your life, or you wish you were still a kid when life was simple? **Nostalgia is great** but if all your best memories were years ago, it's time to start making some fresh ones now.

BE WISE

Relish the fact that as your years increase, so does your wisdom, experience and confidence. So say goodbye to teenage angst and twenty-something low self esteem and **welcome the feelings of calm, sophistication and control.** Celebrate your age instead of denying it.

DON'T WORRY, BE HAPPY

As you get older, you realize that life is too short and some things just aren't worth worrying about. **Don't waste valuable time fretting over things you can't control.** Save that for doing something exciting and fun, you'll feel younger and happier for it!

CHAPTER 6

Happy Home Life

Perfect as Possible

We all want a home that is comfortable to live in, somewhere we can relax and escape from the hustle and bustle of the outside world. On top of that we want a house that we're proud of, and if we're honest, one with the power to impress our friends and family. In short, **all desperate housewives crave one thing – the perfect home.**

And while we secretly know that perfection is impossible, **we're prepared to try our hardest** to achieve as near to that ideal as possible – even with the somewhat limited time and energy we have left after all our work and family commitments.

It is not an easy task, but the key, as with so many things in life, is good organization. A sense of realism is also vital – you need to be able to recognize when you can do a task yourself and **when it makes more sense to delegate** and get in a professional. However, armed with the right advice and a healthy dose of patience, a happy, beautiful home is easily achievable.

How to be a
DÉCOR DIVA

The first step to a fabulous abode is to decorate in a simple but stylish manner. But because **getting started is the hardest part** of doing up a house, here are some tricks to help you on your way.

PICK A
KEY ITEM

When decorating a room from scratch, **don't spend hours looking through paint colour charts** – it can be overwhelming and not very useful. Instead find an inspiring fabric or a great rug and choose a wall colour from the palette it provides.

BE SNAP
HAPPY

Take a digital camera everywhere you go when you're hunting for things for your home. **You'll never find everything you want at one shop,** so taking a picture will help you compare items from different places. Then you can download all your photos onto your computer to help you sort through your selections and envision them all together in your home.

FOLLOW YOUR
OWN STYLE

Design your space how you like it. Choosing trendy furniture or popular styles may seem like a good idea at the time, but six months down the line you could become bored because it is so common – or it could look dated. **Choose things that appeal to you – not anyone else.**

MIX AND
MATCH

Don't be scared to **mix different furniture finishes and styles.** Many people become obsessed with buying furniture in matching sets, but this is not always the most creative or interesting way to design your rooms. Try mixing up the textures and materials. Wood, metal and modern plastic can work really well together and help create a real wow factor.

Clever ROOM DRESSING tricks

Hang pictures and mirrors at eye level for a balanced look.

Use similar frames when hanging pictures in groups to synchronize the look.

When hanging a grouping of pictures on the wall, test out the placing with paper cut to the size of your frame. This will stop you making mistakes and ending up with lots of holes in your walls.

To make a room brighter, hang a mirror on a wall opposite a window to reflect the light.

Keep lamps in a room at the same level. This gives your eye a horizon line and creates an even, calm glow throughout the room.

Decorate nurseries and kids' rooms with their own art. Buy ready-made frames and place their pictures inside. Your kids will love having their work displayed and you will have some great original art in your home.

Do accessories in threes. Three candles grouped together look better than two. Odd numbers always work well for accessorizing.

Fill your rooms with plants. They add an element of life and make a space feel more alive.

Place fresh flowers in every space possible to make rooms appear more inviting. Even one single stem looks effective.

Getting the Help You Need

Whether it's plumbing, painting or just day-to-day cleaning, there will always be times when you need to **call in some extra help.**

For some reason, in this day and age, finding good, honest, reliable professionals that don't charge the earth can seem almost impossible. So, when you're looking to hire someone new, it's always a huge help if you have a friend who can **recommend someone** who they have had a good experience with. Otherwise you could try looking in the local papers or local shops for adverts, or scanning the Internet.

Whatever you do though, never go with the first person you speak to. Call several professionals before deciding which one to hire and always **ask for written quotes** for the job required and check out any references they provide.

With more specialist services, such as electrics or plumbing, you might want to **check if they are registered with an industry institution.** It's also worth finding out if they have adequate insurance, just in case things happen to go wrong.

Compare quotes, but **don't always go for the cheapest option** – especially if it appears substantially lower than all the others. There is usually a reason for a ridiculously low price and you may end up with shoddy work or unreliable workmen. Choosing an estimate somewhere in the middle of all the quotes is often safest.

Most people will require a deposit upfront to buy materials, but **avoid paying the whole cost until the job is finished** and you are satisfied with the work, otherwise you will have no comeback.

If you have problems with the work, calmly explain what the problems are and ask your supplier what they can do to sort them out. If the gentle approach doesn't work and you feel you can't employ them any more, **be firm but polite and send them on their way**. Refuse to pay for the work with which you are unhappy and, if necessary, consider legal action.

When you've chosen the right man for the job, try and get a firm date for when they can start. This can often be quite difficult as many tradesmen are very busy and fit jobs in when they get a spare moment. It helps if you can **confirm a mutually acceptable date** so you know you won't be hanging around for months waiting for the phone to ring.

Call in the
SPECIALISTS

BUILDERS/CONSTRUCTION

Good builders are like gold dust, so if you find
a good one, hang on to him. It's always best to
use builders recommended to you by friends or
family. If you're stuck, try asking neighbours or
other people who live in your street and have
had work done recently.

ELECTRICIANS

Even for the most enthusiastic do-it-yourself
enthusiast, there are **some things that are best
left to the professionals** – in some countries
electrical wiring is actually illegal to do yourself.

INTERIOR DESIGNERS

Architects and interior designers can really help
you get the best out of your home. You may
think they are an expensive luxury, but a once-
only fee **could transform your home** from
something ordinary to something outstanding.

PAINTERS

People often feel guilty calling in painters and
decorators as they see it as a job they can do
themselves. But **if you're time-pressed** and don't
want to give up your evenings and weekends to
do it, it is well worth the money. A painter will
come in and do the job very quickly and usually
with far better results.

GARDENERS

Gorgeous, well-kept gardens can provide hours of pleasure for the whole family. But they can also be **very time-consuming** and take up precious leisure time. A good gardener can do all the difficult, boring jobs like grass cutting and digging, leaving you to worry about which pretty plants to buy.

CATERERS

Whether you're planning an intimate dinner party or a larger affair, **when you want to impress** it's worth hiring a caterer to handle things for you. Most firms will do everything, from preparing and cooking the food to supplying and cleaning the plates and glasses. So you simply have to sit back and be a charming hostess – heaven!

CLEANERS

When you lead a hectic lifestyle, **a good cleaner is a godsend.** They're like little fairies that come in and restore your house to perfection while you're at work. Most cleaning agencies offer a range of services, from a few hours a week to a once-a-year spring clean to give your home a thorough top-to-toe clear-out.

From Desperate Housewife to Domestic Goddess

So you've painted, primped and preened and you love the way your home looks – but only for the first five minutes after the cleaner has been. The rest of the time you feel like your space is overcome by clutter and mess – and you seem to spend the whole time clearing up after your family. Take heart: it is possible to reclaim your rooms from the piles of paperwork and toys. Here is how to **clear up your space and keep it organized – for good.**

How to make a TEAR-FREE TRANSITION to a calmer household

DO A LITTLE AT A TIME

Rather than feeling overwhelmed by the enormous task of clearing the whole house, **make improvements bit by bit** – it will help keep you sane. It is also a great encouragement to watch as things slowly and steadily improve.

BE RUTHLESS

If you feel uncomfortable throwing something away, ask yourself some brutal questions. **'Do I like this item?'**, **'Do I use it?'** and **'Is this the best place for it?'** If you answer no to any of the above, you know the answer – get rid of it. Letting go of things you don't need will clear space for better things to come into your life – materially and emotionally.

PUT CLEARING-UP TIME IN YOUR DIARY

Schedule time to clear your clutter. In fact, put it on your **'to do' list** or on a calendar as an appointment that cannot be missed.

IMAGINE YOUR HOME ORGANIZED

Visualize the way you want to live every day and eventually you will get there.

THROW AWAY BEFORE YOU BUY

Before you go shopping for new clothes, furniture or ornaments, have a clear out and throw away anything you don't want. **It will clear space** and also make you focus on only buying things you really need.

CLEAN AS YOU GO

After you cook, iron or use anything, put it away. It sounds simple, but makes a huge difference. Try to **train your husband and kids** to do the same!

START AN AT-HOME FILING SYSTEM

Prepare a paper organizer for all of your house papers and bills that end up laying around the house. Then separate these sections into areas such as 'credit card', 'electricity' or 'phone bills', so that you end up with an easy-to-access directory of all your paperwork.

MEAL PLANNING

It may sound tedious but it does save time: **pre-plan your evening meals for the week ahead and shop accordingly.** But if you really enjoy cooking, indulge in it over the weekend when you have more time and are relaxed enough to enjoy it. If you dislike cooking, do it just enough to train up your children and partner – one of them might develop a passion for cooking and you'll never need to do it again! Experimenting with unusual dishes will also keep the boredom at bay and provide a challenge.

Contain the Chaos

The amount of mess **increases exponentially** according to how many people live in one space, but there are a few ways to keep everyone's belongings organized and natural chaos under control.

FIX IT IMMEDIATELY

When it's broke, you need to fix it, and fast. **Anything that's not working properly in the home will just get you down, even if it's something as small as a loose doorknob or a leaky tap.** Don't wait to replace lightbulbs or fuses. **Keep a small toolkit handy** for minor repairs.

STORE AND STOW

You can never have enough storage space. **Make sure to utilize under-bed and under-stairs areas** for extra storage and buy stackable cartons for storing out-of-season clothes, children's toys and crafts, or anything you want to keep but don't need to have on display. A dining room table with drawers or a coffee table that doubles as a storage unit are good investments as they can be used to sweep away items in a flash.

KIDS' ROOMS

Organize children's rooms according to where they can reach – actually get down to their level and see if boxes are stacked too high or books are out of reach. **Organize from the floor of the room to the top.** Try to make things easier to put away and harder to get out. Label boxes with both a word and a picture so kids can identify it.

HOME ON THE RANGE

Every object should have a designated home that all family members are aware of. This is key: communicate so no one can claim someone else is 'hiding' things! Keys should go on a key hook near a door, coats on coat racks, and so on. It may seem obvious but if you notice items are not in their 'home station', someone isn't getting the picture.

ESTABLISH A JUNK DRAWER

Have one place where people can **dump any items that don't have a 'home'** or for when they don't know where the 'home' is. Every week, move the items in the junk drawer to their home or establish one if they don't have one.

Living the Luxe Life

When decorating your home or buying any new purchase for it, from a candle to a new sofa, **consider the 'luxury quotient'.** A home that looks, feels and smells wonderful will increase your enjoyment considerably and provide a warm welcome to any guests that visit.

1. **Choose tactile materials** such as leather, sheepskin, cashmere and soft, touchable fabrics for furniture, rugs, pillows and throws. These create a comfortable home that encourages relaxation. Even small touches can be highly effective.

2. **Candles provide light, heat and scent**, warming up a cold room, casting a flattering flickering light, and providing an emotional lift. Larger candles will provide more fragrance as the larger the pool of wax, the more fragrance will evaporate. Fresh flowers not only smell great, but they look indulgent, too.

3. **Mirrors reflect candlelight** and make a small room appear bigger. Gilt frames provide elegance and opulence.

4. **Choose an overall minimalist neutral palette,** and then use colour for accessories to accent the room.

5. **Look at the finish and shape of objects** and keep them all sympathetic – this is more important than having everything from the same time period.

6. **Don't be erratic with the levels** either; go for either a low style of furniture or a high one, but mixing and matching can make a room feel disturbing and unbalanced.

Make Your Bedroom a Boudoir

Your bedroom should be the **one place where you can seek refuge** from the world outside; where you can relax without distractions. After all, how can you really get down to some seriously good sex with a stack of unpaid bills or a pile of dirty socks vying for your attention?

CLEAR THE **CLUTTER**

Stacks of clothes, papers and kids' toys will make it hard for you to get in the mood for rest and romance. So **stash anything that is not relaxation- or love-related** in another room. And keep laundry – dirty or clean – hidden away in the closet.

KEEP LIGHTING **SOFT AND SEXY**

The lighting in the perfect bedroom should generally be soft and low wattage. **Consider installing a dimmer switch for your overhead light,** so you can change the mood of the room easily. Ditch unflattering bright lights in favour of table lamps. Of course, the glow of candlelight is the sexiest and most flattering form of illumination. To symbolize a happy and warm relationship, try placing two candles close together. And if they're scented, even better – in the bedroom, it's best to stick to headier aromas, like musk and vanilla.

BETTER **BED**

The bed is the centrepiece of your bedroom. **Buy the biggest one that you can afford** that will fit into your room. Nothing beats having a large bed to roll around on. To spice up your existing bed, try adding a romantic bed tent or canopy. Or turn it into a four-poster by purchasing a four-poster bed frame.

TRY **PILLOW** TALK

There is nothing more sensual and inviting than a
bed covered with bolsters and fluffy pillows. Make
your bed a place your partner will never want to
leave by buying **the softest down pillows and
silkiest sheets.** Even though good sheets are
more expensive, it's well worth it. Choose soft
fabrics like jersey or brushed cotton.

SCENTS AND SENSUALITY

Your nose is connected to the limbic system
of the brain, which controls your libido. This is
why certain **scents can evoke specific moods or
memories** and can also get you in the mood for
love. Try adding several drops of your favourite
aromatherapy oil to the softener section of your
washing machine when you wash your sheets
in hot water. Another trick is to fill a spray bottle
with water and add a few drops of your favourite
oil or perfume and then spray it on your sheets.
The scent will last for weeks.

STRIKE A **BALANCE**

According to Feng Shui you should **keep each
side of your bed even.** In other words, if you
have a table and lamp on your side, make sure
there's one on his side, too – even if there
currently is no him. The idea being that it sends
out very subtle signals that you are ready to have
a partner in your life and that you have a space
for him, both literally and figuratively.

How to Host the
Perfect Dinner Party

Throwing a great dinner party is one of those things every self-respecting, sophisticated housewife thinks she should be able to do – and with style and aplomb. Sadly, it's not quite as easy as all that. **From deciding what to cook to who to invite, the task can be fraught with pitfalls.**

Many of us end up, Bridget-Jones-style, using every pan we possess in an effort to replicate some pretentious creation in a glossy cookbook, only to find ourselves with a **complete food disaster** on our hands. It is one of life's strange facts that having a few people over for dinner can turn the most reasonable individual into a gibbering mess.

But it doesn't have to be so hard. The trick is to create the illusion that several Michelin-starred chefs have been slaving behind the scenes to produce, when in fact, you whipped the whole thing up in ten minutes before you left for work.

KNOW YOUR GUESTS

If the dinner party is an informal affair with friends, this shouldn't be a problem. But if it is business related and more formal, try to **find out any extreme likes and dislikes,** and if any of the guests are vegetarian, have specific dietary requirements or any allergies.

KEEP IT SIMPLE

Follow the advice of top chefs and **cook simple, tasty food** well. If possible, ensure one dish is a cold one so that you're not constantly clock-watching. Never bite off more than you can chew by trying to cook a complicated dish that you haven't served before – it's best to be familiar with any potential pitfalls or difficult ingredients.

PREPARE, PREPARE, PREPARE

After all, you're the host and should spend as much time with your guests as possible. If you seem flustered or always rushing about, people will feel uncomfortable. You can **do a lot before the guests arrive** – serve up cold appetizers and refrigerate desserts. Get sauces ready. And be sure to lay the table and put out a few nibbles before people start to arrive.

BE COMPLEMENTARY

Plan courses that go well with each other, and **don't repeat ingredients throughout the courses.**

DON'T PILE UP PLATES

Your guests will feel awkward and think they have to eat it all if there's too much food on their plates. You may want to serve the main ingredient, say meat or fish, and pass the vegetables around separately. But **make more sauce than you think you'll need** – people always ask for more.

DIVE IN

If the dinner party is an informal gathering with friends, a buffet is a brilliant way to keep a dinner party hassle-free. **Create a selection of interesting dishes** – hot and cold – place on the table and let everybody grab what they want. Tapas, fondue and sushi are all great choices for easy, intimate hands-on dining.

CHOOSE THE RIGHT WINE

If you're not sure, **ask your local wine shop for advice,** telling them what you're serving and asking for a recommendation that suits the food and your budget. And be sure to offer mineral water with the meal.

THE ROOM

Make sure your house looks clean and tidy, and smells sweet. **Candles, flowers and fairy lights will all help to add the perfect finishing touches.** And be imaginative – if you have a tiny dining table, or don't own one at all, then use comfy floor pillows for an exotic, informal feel.

ENJOY YOURSELF

A glass of wine relaxes you in stressful situations. Just be careful that a glass doesn't turn into a bottle until after you've finished cooking! **But as soon as the food hits the table, relax.** Don't forget, as well as giving you the chance to impress with your culinary skills, the reason you invited people was to enjoy their company. The best parties are the ones where the hostess relaxes and enjoys herself, and doesn't try to run it like a military operation. So, go on, have some fun!

Throwing a Good Party

Many of the same rules for dinner parties are relevant for casual entertaining, though it's all more relaxed. Without the structure of the dining table, mixing is much more flowing and informal. Here are some **tips to make everyone feel more comfortable,** whether you are hosting an impromptu supper for a couple of friends, a tailgate party at a sports event, a big birthday bash or a summer barbecue.

1. **Invitations** should be sent out at least one month before the event. RSVPs should be returned two weeks before the event.

2. **Rent chairs and tables** if you do not have enough. Assess the venue to see how many seating possibilities there actually are.

3. **Organize the food** on a rota basis so when one tray (of appetizers, crudités or food for the barbecue) is finished, you can bring out a back-up. Each should have the same diverse range.

4. **Keep an eye out for solo guests** and stragglers, working the area to bring them into contact with others. Your goal should be that everyone is engaged.

5. **Always have enough drinks for teetotallers** – don't just assume that everyone will be happy with wine or beer.

6. **Introduce new people** to your circle of friends. What you give out, comes back.

7. **Notify your neighbours.** This is essential if you intend having a barbecue or garden party.

8. **Choose finger foods** without messy sauces. Make sure they complement each other.

9. **Always have more food** and drink than you think you need, enough glassware and tea/coffee for the end of the evening.

10. **Expect that accidents will happen** so you aren't upset when they do – this is all part of being prepared. Don't run around trying to clean up – it's not in the spirit of the party and you'll look like a neurotic housewife.

11. **Music is essential** – it helps provide background noise at the beginning when there are fewer people, it can be a conversation starter and it's available if anyone chooses to dance.

12. **Plan for the end.** Have a number of a taxi company available for those who need a way home.

Dealing With Difficult House Guests

FIND OUT
WHAT YOU'RE IN FOR

Once you know exactly how many people are coming and how long they're staying, you can prepare yourself mentally. **Don't be shy to ask.** If you find this awkward, pretend that you're planning on going away or expecting other guests and need to get organized. Not knowing how many people are going to descend on you or how long they're planning to stay is extremely stressful. It's your home and you have a right to know these things in advance. The last thing you want is Uncle Bob coming for two weeks and staying for two years. Stranger things have happened.

ROPE THE FAMILY
IN TO HELP

Washing and ironing, food shopping and cleaning are all time-consuming tasks. So **get your partner and/or kids to help you** the day before the guests arrive. This will ensure you're not feeling stressed out and exhausted before they've even rung the doorbell. If you have a cleaner, get them to do extra hours the day before or change the day to fit in with your guests.

DON'T PROVIDE
ROUND-THE-CLOCK ENTERTAINMENT

Assuming full responsibility for your guests' daily schedule and needs will drive you round the bend. It's also up to them to make some effort to keep occupied – especially if you're working. **Let guests go off and do their own thing** for some of the time and don't fall into the trap of becoming unofficial tour guide, clown and general skivvy. You will be burnt out within a day or two. So make some 'me time' for yourself and your partner. Pop out shopping or for lunch – and don't feel guilty!

KEEP YOUR
ROUTINES

Obviously things will be a little different when you have a house full of people, but if you usually go to bed at 10 pm, don't suddenly sit up until midnight and expect to function normally the next day. **Your guests should fit in with your living arrangements.**

The same goes for regular classes, meetings or other social events – keep them up. As long as you tell your guests beforehand, then you're not being rude. Of course you should be making time for your guests and trying to make their stay as enjoyable as possible – just not to the point that it disrupts your entire life, or resentment will start to creep in.

GET GUESTS
HELPING

Feeding hungry guests three times a day can be stressful, to say the least – not to mention tiring. **Prepare as much as possible beforehand by cooking and freezing meals,** and don't be frightened to ask guests to cook some meals themselves, especially if they're staying for more than a couple of days. And if they're not forthcoming in washing up – ask them to do it! Often guests will ask 'Is there anything I can do to help?' and instead of politely saying no, take them up on their offer and delegate some chores.

SEND THEM
SHOPPING

Buying food for twice the normal number of people is a major hassle and **can become very expensive.** While we all like to treat family and friends, if people come to stay for more than a weekend, you cannot be expected to pay for all their living expenses. Make a list and ask them to go to the supermarket for you – chances are they will offer to pay for all, or at least half the bill.

REMEMBER
WHOSE HOUSE IT IS

If your kids are not allowed to jump on the sofa, then theirs shouldn't either. Don't be scared to enforce regular bed-times or mealtimes, especially if your kids are used to it. If there are things that are important to you, it is much better to **say so at the beginning of the stay** before it becomes a problem. It is your home and people in it need to respect your rules.

PROTECT
YOUR HOME

Make sure you **hide anything precious away** if your guests have small children. Do this in advance so you don't spend the whole stay rescuing DVDs and expensive ornaments from their grabbing hands. Pack away breakables that are at eye- or ankle-level and lock the cupboard that contains your TV or CD player.

JUST
SAY NO

The final thing to remember about playing host is **not to feel that you have to be at the beck and call of every suggestion** your guests make. If you want to hit the sack and they want to hit the town, let them go on their own. Or if their children want to spend hours on the Internet or playing loud pop music, you have a right to say when enough is enough!

Keeping Up With the Jones's

There she goes again – swanning about in her Prada dress and Gucci heels with her tall, dark and handsome husband and her three beautiful kids. When a glamorous woman moves into your neighbourhood, with a perfect life to boot, it can leave you feeling a bit inadequate. But beware: there is **no more destructive emotion than jealousy.** Here's how to defuse those feelings of neighbourly inferiority.

ACCEPT THAT EVERYONE HAS THEIR PLUS POINTS

People are born with different strengths and weaknesses. Some are clever, some are thin, some are pretty, some have lots of friends and some have creative talents – whatever. People are not the same and they themselves often have little to do with the good things life has sent their way. You most probably have things of which she is jealous. **Don't beat yourself up about it.**

DON'T COMPARE

There will always be people who are better off, prettier, more successful than you, but the reverse is also true. Comparisons serve no function, except to make you desperately unhappy. **Try to be content with what you have and delight in it**. If you are discontent, try to discover what lies beneath the feeling. Often it reveals much more about your feelings of inadequacy than with the object of your jealousy. Self-help techniques, such as positive thinking and cognitive behavioural therapy, may help you learn to feel good about yourself.

AVOID THE
MATERIALISM TRAP

If your neighbour or best friend buys a yacht, goes on an exotic holiday, or attains some obvious sign of increased wealth or success, try to **wish them well without the need to better them.** Competition is healthy if it spurs you on to make something of yourself, but if the goal is to buy more 'things', it could be that you need to re-examine your personal value system and what makes you happy.

TAKE SOLACE IN BEING
FINANCIALLY SOUND

Console yourself with the fact that **you are spending within your means.** You might not have that new TV and convertible car, but you're not going to go bankrupt either.

NOBODY'S LIFE
IS PERFECT

No one's life is plain sailing from start to finish – we all hit problems and turbulent times. She may have all the money in the world, but her husband might ignore her when no one is around to see it. Her career may be great, but one of her children could have learning disabilities. You may not know these things. **Don't make yourself miserable by just looking at the façade** she chooses to present to the world. The brand new car may have been bought entirely on credit or the recent career change may not be anywhere near as happy as she makes it sound.

BE FRIENDLY

Don't see all contact as a competition. **Make it clear that you're not going to play that game** – others can't compete all on their own. You will meet people who boast about their achievements, acquisitions, children's successes, and so on. The best way to deal with this is to smile nicely, look bored and chat about things you are both interested in.

Settling into a New Neighbourhood

Moving home, especially when it's to a brand new area, is **one of the most stressful things you will ever do.** Just thinking about uprooting your family by selling your home, finding a new place to live, packing and settling in can raise the most tranquil person's blood pressure to dangerous levels. So many decisions, so much uncertainty, so many adjustments... But your attitude toward a move often has a great influence on how smoothly the process goes.

If you are faced with this daunting prospect, try to look at it as a fantastic opportunity to live in a new place. See it as an adventure. It's not easy to make a new neighbourhood feel like home, but with time and effort the rewards are always worth the short-term upheaval. The following steps will help things run as smoothly as possible.

GET SORTED

Creating an ordered home should be your first priority. Unpacking will seem less of a daunting task if you break it down into manageable chunks and don't try to do everything at once. **Make a list of what needs to be done.** See it as a great opportunity to have a perfectly organized home, however briefly, before the inevitable clutter starts to accumulate!

FOOD FIRST

Start by unpacking kitchen items so food and drink won't be a problem, as lack of food is a sure-fire reason for people to feel grumpy. Don't worry about making dinner your first night – **try out one of your new local takeouts.**

SLEEP EASY

Make up the beds as soon as possible. If you are able to sleep in your own bed and **have a good breakfast,** you'll be in better shape to deal with the task ahead.

HELP THE KIDS SETTLE IN

The more that children are involved in the moving process, the less disruptive and worrying it will seem. Making new surroundings seem familiar is vital, so pack a box with all your kids' special toys and belongings, and unpack these straight away. **Involve your children** in planning how to decorate their new bedrooms.

BEGIN TO EXPLORE

Once normal routines have been re-established, children can start exploring further. Give older kids back-up emergency phone numbers and encourage them to learn as much about the new area as they can before moving. If possible, take your children to **visit their new schools and meet the teachers.**

FINDING CHILDCARE

One of the first things to do is to find childcare in the area. **Search the local papers, ask other parents or carers for recommendations** and consider local play groups, nurseries and nanny or babysitting agencies. If you need help only occasionally, you may find a babysitting circle where one of the parents babysit the neighbourhood children on a rota basis.

FIVE TIPS for making
MOVING EASIER
for the kids

1 **Set up the kids' rooms first.** This gives them a sense of familiarity as well as a place to relax, unpack or play while the rest of the unpacking is going on in the house.

2 **Take short walks** around the neighbourhood. This is a great way to meet new neighbours and potential friends.

3 **Draw a neighbourhood map** with your children indicating the locations of the school, playground, park and shops. This will make them feel more confident about finding their way around a new area.

4 **Check out local groups** your family may have been involved with in your former community – churches, sports, social or cultural organizations and activities.

5 **Arrange a tour of your child's school.** As well as classrooms, be sure to find the library, cafeteria, playgrounds and bus stop.

Making NEW friends

★ Encourage youngsters to join in local activities. This
is probably the best way to meet new friends. These
could include a sports team, special-interest club, Scouts,
playgroup, and so on. At the same time, help them keep
in touch with their old friends.

★ Set up play dates with colleagues from work or families
from your new area for younger children to meet and
get to know each other.

★ Find activities for your school-age children to join in
with, such as sports teams, clubs, lessons and classes.
Meeting kids with the same interests increases their
chances of finding a friend.

★ Take the initiative and introduce yourself to the
neighbours. Your kids' – or your – new best friends
may literally be living next door.

★ Offer to buy your new neighbours a drink or coffee if
you see them out at a local place or social event. This
way you can establish a speaking relationship while they
can acquaint you with who's who.

★ When you feel more settled, invite your immediate
neighbours, especially those with children, to a
barbecue or informal dinner so that the kids can get
to know each other in a relaxed atmosphere.

★ When you are invited to do things, say 'yes' even
though you feel shy, don't know how to get to the
hostesses house, or don't know what to wear.

Neighbours from Hell and What to Do About Them

It's Monday night, it's past midnight but it seems unlikely you'll be getting any sleep for the next couple of hours. You wouldn't mind too much normally, but having spent the last two nights wide awake as your neighbours partied into the night, **you're just about ready to kill them.** Your heart is thumping, your stress levels are going through the roof and you are having visions of violent ways in which you can achieve silence.

Having the neighbours from hell is a nightmare – and can cause huge amounts of stress. Whether it is a barking dog, a messy front garden or even somebody doing do-it-yourself in the middle of the night, it can disrupt yours and your family's life – **so what can you do?**

Get to know your neighbours when they move in. It is easier to sort out problems if you have met each other on neutral or friendly ground already.

Talk to your neighbour when the noise gets too much to bear. It might be a bit difficult but often people do not realize they are making a noise and will happily change their routine so you are not bothered. If you are worried that they might get angry if you complain, ask someone to go with you for back up.

Write notes, if the problem continues for more than a week or gets worse, on when it started, how it escalated and what was causing it. If you have conversations with your neighbour, make sure you write them down, too.

Make sure you are not a noisy neighbour before complaining about others. It's important to remember that you might be making noise, too. If you can hear your neighbour, it's likely that they can hear you.

The kids and the dog next door are unaware of you and your desire for silence. Accept that people are often blind to the faults of their pets and their children. Although it might not feel that way, they are not deliberately taunting you.

If all else fails, ask the relevant authorities to visit your house to hear the noise for themselves and if they agree it's too loud, they will issue a notice to the neighbour, which could result in court action if they do not resolve the problem.

What if they do something to you? If you are too scared to complain, either to the neighbours or to the authorities for fear of retribution against you or your property, it might be time to consider moving.

Be a good neighbour yourself. Tell the people in your street when you are planning a party, whether it's a big celebration for your 40th birthday or a fancy dress party for your toddler. If people are forewarned, they are less likely to complain. It also makes them feel as if you are considering their needs and sets the tone for the neighbourhood.

Be careful. Don't underestimate the levels of viciousness to which neighbourly conflicts can escalate. Neighbours who fire shots at each other or poison each other's pets are rare, but not unheard of. If you can't – or don't want to – move, think of getting in a mediator before things turn nasty.

Boost Your Social Life

When you're in your 20s, nightclubs and bars are where the action is and you can't get enough of them. But once you pass the age of 30 **your taste in social activities evolves** somewhat. You become more demanding about how you spend your free time and smoky bars, where you can't get a seat and spend most of the night being jostled around, simply don't hold the same appeal.

At the same time, your middle years can be some of the busiest – leaving you so exhausted that all you can do is collapse on the sofa at the end of another frenetic day. But don't let your daily life deprive you of social time. Getting out of the house and engaging with others, whether you are married or single, have children or not, is **important for everyone's mental health.**

Arrange to meet friends straight from work rather than going home first – it's too tempting to hibernate once you're in, especially during the winter, and harder to extricate yourself from family demands. **Organize childcare for one day a week every week** so you have an evening out to look forward to. When you have children at home it's all too easy to go weeks and months without going out in the evening. Try to make it a day you go out with your partner, but also take advantage of being part of a couple by setting 'girls' and 'boys' nights, where you can each go out alone with friends while the other looks after the children.

Where to GO OUT
when you're over 35

Use your imagination to make the evening more interesting. Instead of just arranging to go to the same old place, research venues and events – surprise your friends or partner with somewhere different. Not only will you be doing something new, and possibly learning something in the process, but it is also good for your personal growth and mental stimulation.

FOCUS ON YOUR
PERSONAL INTERESTS

Try a new group, sport or hobby that interests you and book a series of classes or join a club. It can be anything from a tennis club or amateur dramatics to a language or art class. You'll automatically have a common interest with the people you meet and quickly widen your social circle. **Only consider those that really interest you** and that involve group situations so you get to meet new people. Arrive early to allow time to chat with others and don't be in a rush to leave after class – suggest getting together with your classmates for a cup of coffee afterwards.

BE A **CULTURE**
VULTURE

Keep a lookout for an interesting exhibition, concert or film première to attend. Many museums and art galleries offer evening viewings and have a restaurant or bar you can go along to either before or after. **Or plan a night out at the theatre** to catch that play you've being reading great reviews about.

TEMPT YOUR
PALATE

Enlist a food buddy – either a friend or partner – and make a decision to check out four or five restaurants you've always fancied visiting. An evening of fine wine, good food and great company is **an excellent way to unwind after a busy day** at work – and you might find you develop a new interest in cuisine or wine tasting.

TAKE A **HIKE**

The simple things in life can be the biggest pleasures. **On a beautiful day, nothing beats a walk.** The calming sound of leaves rustling, birds singing and the whole feeling of getting back to nature. It's also great exercise and gets you outdoors.

GET FIT
WITH FRIENDS

Book an exercise class with friends in advance or sign up to a course so you can't back out at the last minute. **Any team sport can make a good social occasion** but most other activities and sports also stimulate interaction.

When You're on Child Duty

As much as you love your children, there's no need to give up adult company because you are with them 24/7. There are ways to organize social activities that are just as much fun for adults as for the children.

FAMILY GET-TOGETHERS

Organize a family reunion. Your kids can have fun with their cousins while you reminisce with your siblings, aunts and uncles.

DAY TRIPPING

Get out of town for the day with another family. Go to the beach, on a woodland walk, to a historical spot, on a bike ride at a nature reserve, or anywhere you've never been before. **Most friends are only too eager to join in,** especially if they are in a similar situation with children. The children will get to spend time together and so will the adults.

WEEKEND **GUESTS**

If your home is big enough, have another family to stay for the weekend. This does not have to be a stressful event, but to make it as laidback as possible, don't worry about having enough for everyone to do. You will find that the children make their own fun and the adults will be happy enough just having their children entertained. For a real treat, **book a hotel or mini-break with another family.** The children can then participate in any activities on offer while the adults socialize.

STAY HOME, BUT **NOT ALONE**

If you really can't face heading out or can't afford a babysitter on a regular basis, **invite friends over to your place and make a night of it** there. Spice up the evening by giving it a theme, such as Moroccan, and ask guests to bring something to contribute like music, food and drink. Organize a girls' night in, centred around a poker game, film night or beauty session where you discuss the latest fashion and make-up trends. Pack your man off to his pals for the night and he'll be happy, too.

Social Life After Divorce

After a marriage break up it's normal to be left feeling a bit battered and bruised, and often **the thought of socializing again can be very daunting.** You might not be comfortable seeing old friends who remind you of the past, while the thought of meeting new people terrifies you.

If you have kids, hanging out with them can be a good way to ease yourself back into the scene. You could **start your own social group** by inviting all your single-parent friends and their children to an event, such as a picnic or a day at the zoo. If you don't know any other single parents, a divorce support group is an excellent place to start. If you don't have kids then your time is now your own – enjoy it!

It's vital to set aside time for these outings – whether it's meeting friends, going to support groups or even on dates. Both you and your kids will reap the benefits as you'll be calmer and happier, which will make you a better parent. **Once a week is a minimum goal** for getting out with another adult, whether you see a movie, exercise together, spend some time window shopping, take a walk or meet for lunch. Making a resolution to enjoy adult interaction on a regular basis will keep you from feeling isolated and lonely; it will also improve your social network so you feel more supported and stable.

Quick Tips for
Child Management

Raising your children so they become responsible, caring, thoughtful individuals is every parent's dream, but the actual process can be every parent's nightmare. Follow these **simple rules to keep your child under control** and get the best behaviour you can out of them – it may not last, but try to realize it's an ongoing process.

1 **Don't expect perfection** – from yourself or others. Give praise for small miracles and special efforts, and modify family rules according to the situation.

2 **Respect your children** and don't try to force them into behaving in a way that is at odds with their personality. You won't get an outgoing, active child to behave like a quiet, shy one no matter what you do.

3 **Keep control and don't over-react.** If your children see you lose it, they are likely to feel unstable, too. They will copy your behaviour quickly, so examine how you react to situations.

4 **Provide for your child's everyday needs.** Give then exercise when they're restless, sleep when they're overtired or fraught, food when they're hungry, and include a good mix of social and quiet time. When their physical needs are met, they are more likely to behave well.

5 **Pay no attention to what other people think** of your child or your parenting skills. Every child can behave like a monster or an angel, so don't get too hung up on what other people think – tantrums are usually over in a flash; sadly, so is polite behaviour.

6 **Reward good behaviour,** penalise bad behaviour. Use star charts, token systems, time-outs and other parenting programmes to reinforce this.

OTHER
PEOPLE'S KIDS

Your children are enough work, so how do you **cope with their friends?**

- If the child is in your home or you are the sole parent in charge, your rules apply. Firm, gentle reminders are often enough – children who misbehave at home usually behave perfectly well at someone else's house. A simple 'Sorry, we don't say (do) that in our house' should suffice.
- Don't try to raise the other child. Instead stick to the problem that's at hand, working toward a solution where everyone benefits.
- Children have frequent arguments and raise their voices. If this begins to escalate, ask them if you can help solve their problem; otherwise leave them to sort it out as it may simply blow over.
- Be as fair as possible when there are disagreements and avoid taking sides.
- If the child does act against the house rules, remind him or her that it's not allowed in the home, but always offer an alternative.

SLEEPOVER
GUIDELINES

You want your children to have fun but you would also like to get some sleep yourself. Here are some **rules to ensure a good time** for children of any age.

- Have an even number of children – odd pairings mean someone is always left out. Limit the number, too: even just four kids can sound and feel like eight.
- Explain the rules of the house to everyone.
- Ask every child's parents about allergies, food requests and sleeptime rituals.
- Devote an entire room to the sleepover. If the child's bedroom is big enough, this is ideal; if not, make it a room with a door.
- Have a 'lights off' time – otherwise you are looking at an all-night party. Don't assume a movie will calm them down – the 'lights off' should also mean all stimulation is off.
- Ensure you have full contact details of parents, children know exactly what they are expected to bring and other parents are informed of the pick-up time.
- Have more food, drink and games than you think you need.

SIBLING

RIVALRY

Children can really fight rough. Whether it's catty bickering or full-on, knock-down fisticuffs, the effects can range from annoying to terrifying. **Try to keep in mind that it's natural for children to fight**. It teaches them important lessons, such as how to argue effectively, understand another's perspective and control impulses. That said, it is helpful to control the conflict, and here's how:

- Recognize why your children are arguing and try to solve the cause, not the symptom. They could be bored, frustrated, not feeling well or anxious.
- Sibling harmony reflects harmony in the whole household. Look at the way everyone in the family treats each other and you might see a mirror of this in the children's behaviour.
- Separate the children until they are calm. Ask them to come up with a solution to the problem individually and then discuss it.
- Don't focus on who did what. It takes two to tango and it's likely both are to blame.
- If the children are arguing over possessions. make a schedule so that each one has a fair share of time using the toy, computer, game, or whatever it is.
- Avoid dismissing anyone's feelings. Acknowledge the anger and then encourage working through it.
- Allow them to find their own solutions. Usually it is best to stay out of it so that they can learn how to resolve their differences.

Fun for All the Family

Family time is the hardest to prioritize because the demands of work and household chores always seem more urgent. However, **it's the most precious time you have,** and the time that matters most of all. If you and your partner both work, it's important to make the most of the time you have together with your children.

The best tip for making your family time count is to guard it carefully – and make it fun. As your children grow, you'll find there are **ever-increasing and conflicting demands on everyone's time.** Supposedly free time can be taken up with your work and their social life. You'll soon find that if you don't mark out some time to spend as a family, it won't happen. Here's how to maximize fun time and spend as much time together as possible.

DIARY 'TOGETHER TIME'

You need to plan family activities ahead and make them clear to everyone. Put them in the diary or calendar and make sure everyone understands that this is precious time and you don't want the plans changed. Don't worry if you haven't actually decided where you're going on Saturday afternoon – just **make sure the whole family knows something's happening.**

As your kids grow up, **make it clear to them how much you value time spent together** by talking about it. Tell them that Saturday afternoons with the family mean a lot to you – they'll appreciate that you want to be with them and ditch last-minute invites from their friends accordingly.

DON'T BE DISTRACTED

Avoid the temptation to answer your mobile and, if you're at home, put the answering machine on. If your job involves taking phone calls at home, don't be at the beck and call of every little query. Serious problems have to be dealt with, but you shouldn't be bothered lots of times over the weekend or during the evening.

MAKE THE MOST OF IT

Never underestimate how much you can get out of just a few moments' one-to-one time with your kids. Even babies know and appreciate when they're being fully engaged with and **enjoyed for their own sake.** As they grow up, nothing makes kids feel more special than a few moments of their parents' undivided attention.

KID-FRIENDLY Activities

Children crave entertainment, but the most important thing to remember when looking for the 'perfect family activity' is that there isn't any such thing! You'll enjoy your time with your children and vice versa if you **relax and just have fun.**

Here are a few things to try.

ROLLERBLADING

Cheap and fun, plus many rinks have a family night. If you make this a regular outing, buy them their own pair of blades.

PICNICS

It doesn't have to be a special occasion, **just pack a bag of food** and go to your nearest park, throw down a rug and enjoy. Kids always love eating outdoors and it means they can run around and play at the same time.

GAMES NIGHT

I know that often after a hard day's work we just want to sit, relax and do nothing. But, once you get into the habit of designating one evening a week 'Family Games Night' you'll all start to look forward to it. It's **fun, educational and provides an opportunity for conversation.** Choose board games or word games that everyone enjoys.

MUSEUMS

Even if you live in the sticks you'll be able to find a museum within reasonable distance. **Do some research** to discover the most interesting attractions in your area.

GET THEM TO TEACH YOU SOMETHING

Whether it's how to play the latest video game or the words to their favourite songs, it's a great way to bond with your kids and let them know that you care about what they like. **Don't be afraid to look silly** while you try the things they enjoy.

COOKING

Many children are quite keen on learning how to cook – and teaching them can have the dual benefit of meaning you have help getting dinner ready. If you've instilled a **healthy love of cooking** in them, they'll be able to give you a night off dinner duty on a regular basis!

Useful Websites

www.awomansresource.com/careerwomen.html
A community for career women. How to land that perfect job, and more...

www.bettersleep.org
The official site from the Better Sleep Council – start sleeping better tonight.

www.goodhousekeeping.co.uk/reader_questions.html
Expert advice on running your home from the Good Housekeeping Institute.

www.health-fitness-tips.com
Latest in-the-zone information for your health and fitness.

www.howtolookgood.com
Fashion and style solutions so every woman can look fabulous.

www.mumsnet.com
Practical parenting – product reviews, antenatal clubs, contacts in your area; discuss anything from movies to mother-in-laws.

www.relate.org.uk
Advice, relationship counselling, sex therapy, workshops, mediation, consultations and support face-to-face, by phone and via this website.